ART ZONE

By

Orlando Hernandez

DESCRIPTION

"You have to wait until after you die in order to become a famous artist," is what people often told me. Well, it's a good thing that I don't listen to people!!! No, I don't expect to be famous ... Hey!! Being infamous is just fine with me ... but that would be missing the whole point.

The truth of the matter is that I suffer from this rare disease ... it's called having to eat every day. And we all know that you would not want me to go hungry just because that's what starving artists do. So let's forget about fame and let's think about food!!! Feel free to give me a job so that I can eat.

This book is composed of murals (completed and current) in hopes of securing a meal. This book is my last human attempt (bots standing by) at pleading with those of you who not only have a heart, but also happen to be art lovers. Now is the time!! Give me a job today!!! And don't wait until I'm dead.

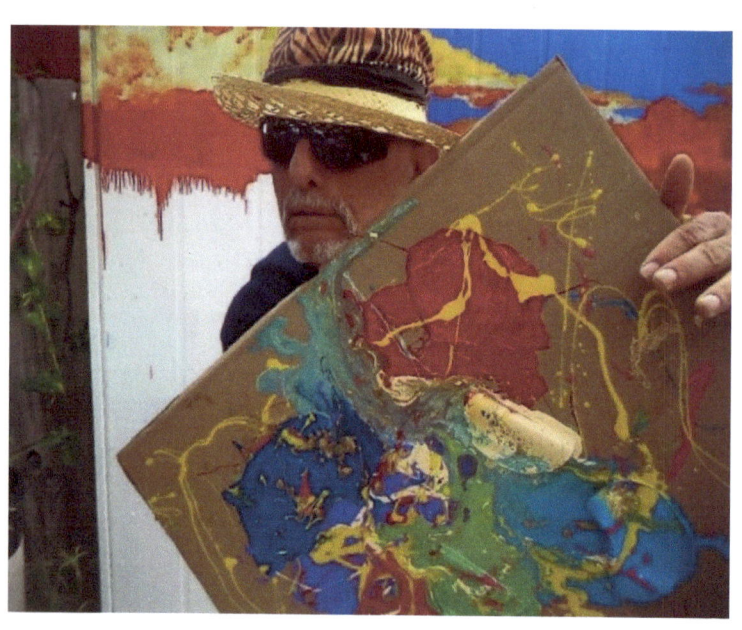

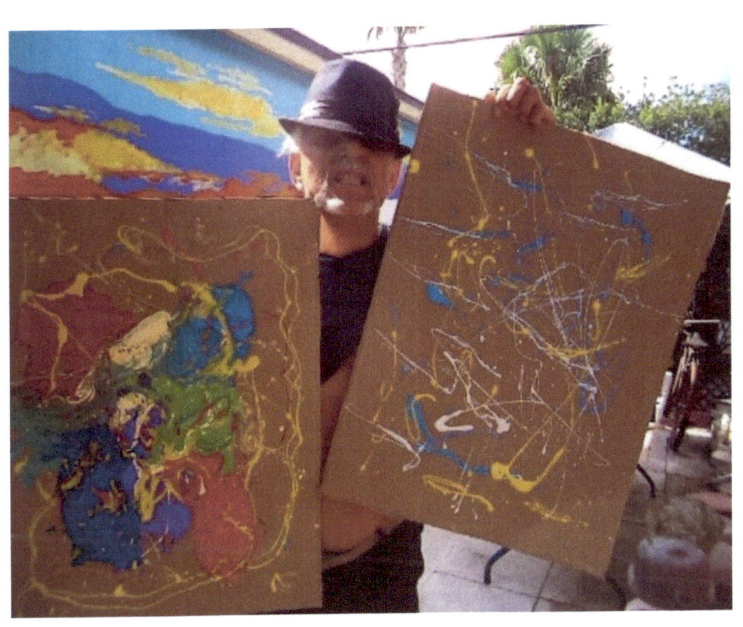

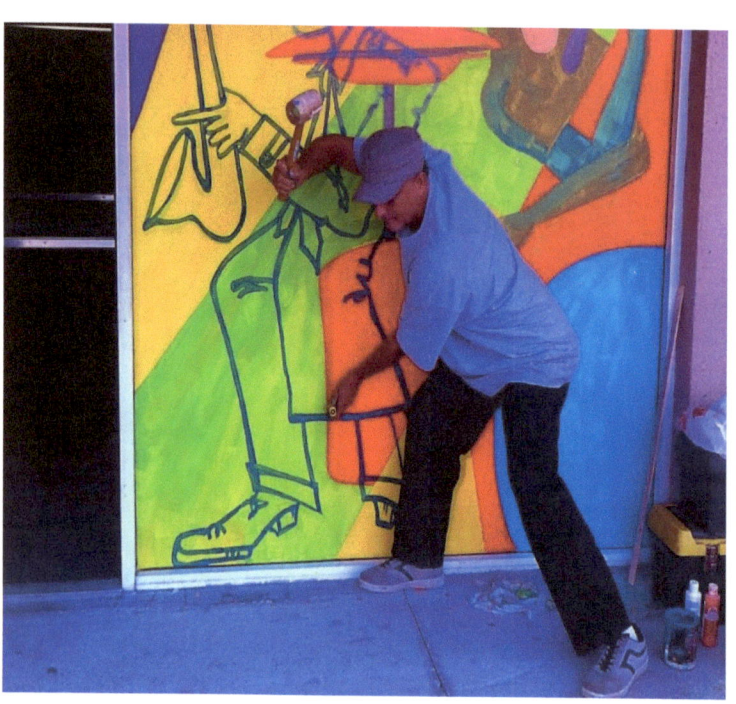

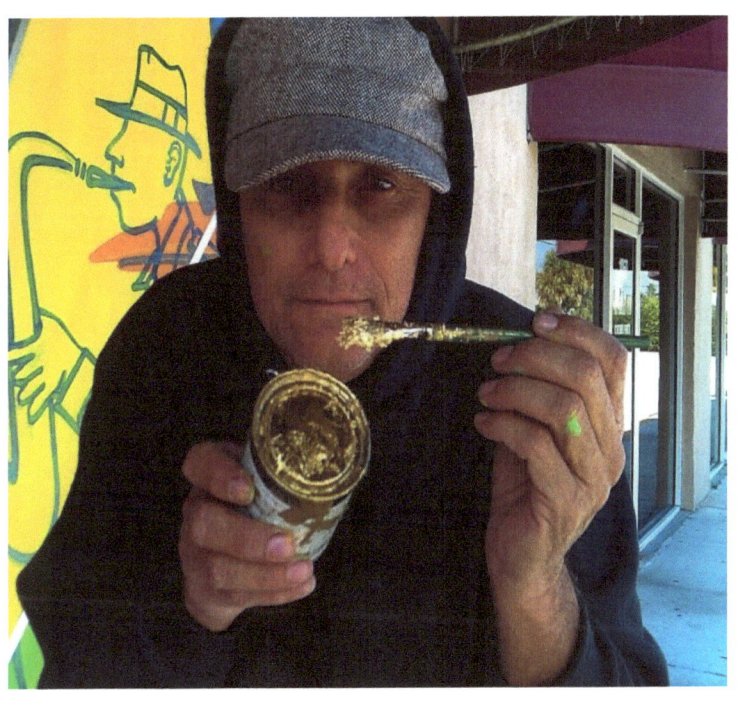

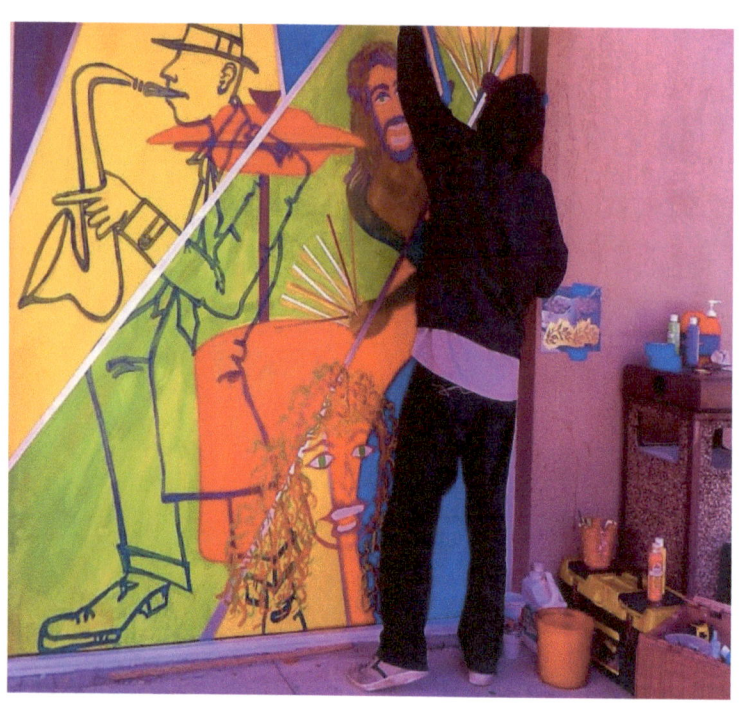

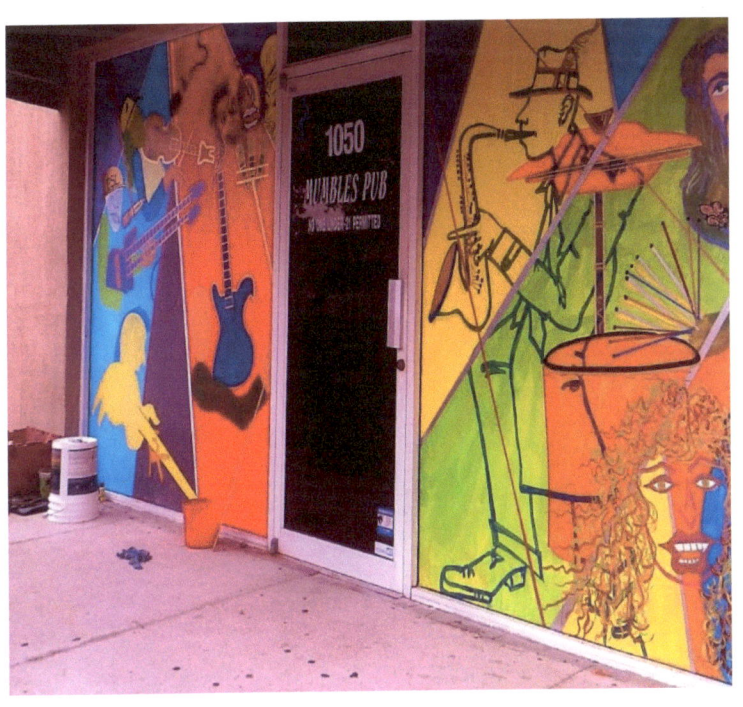

7

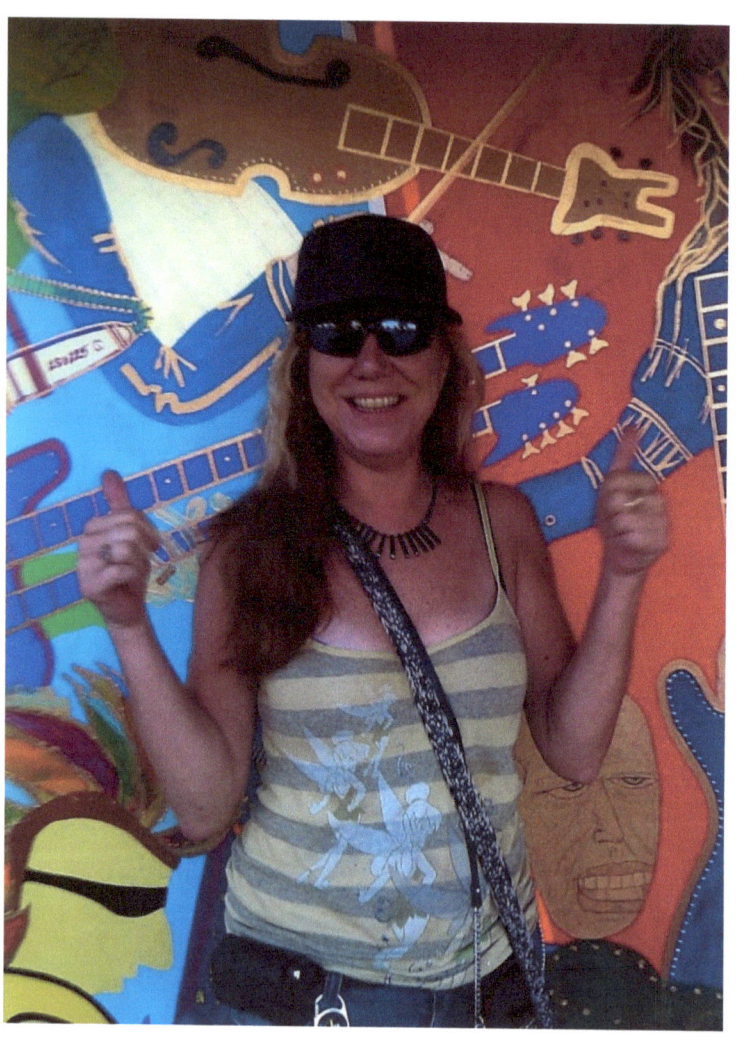

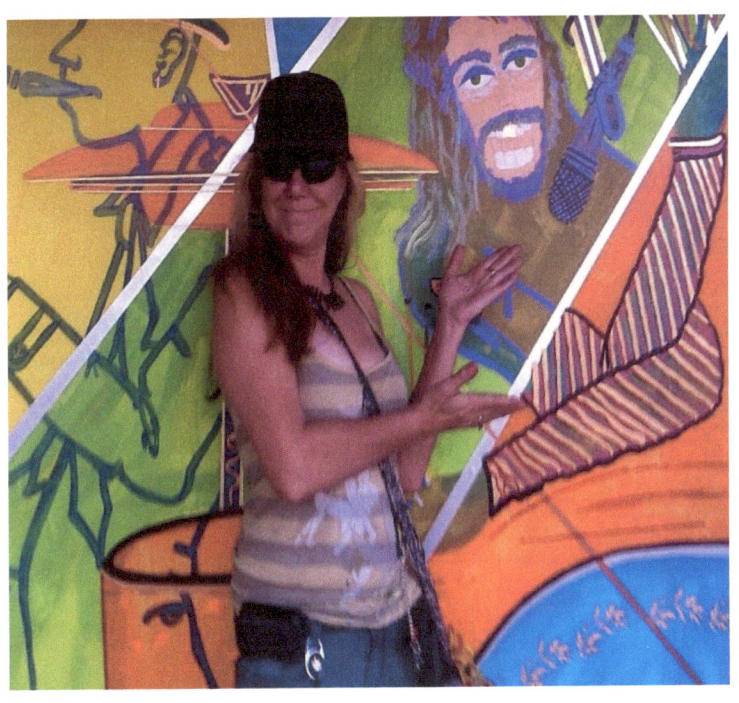

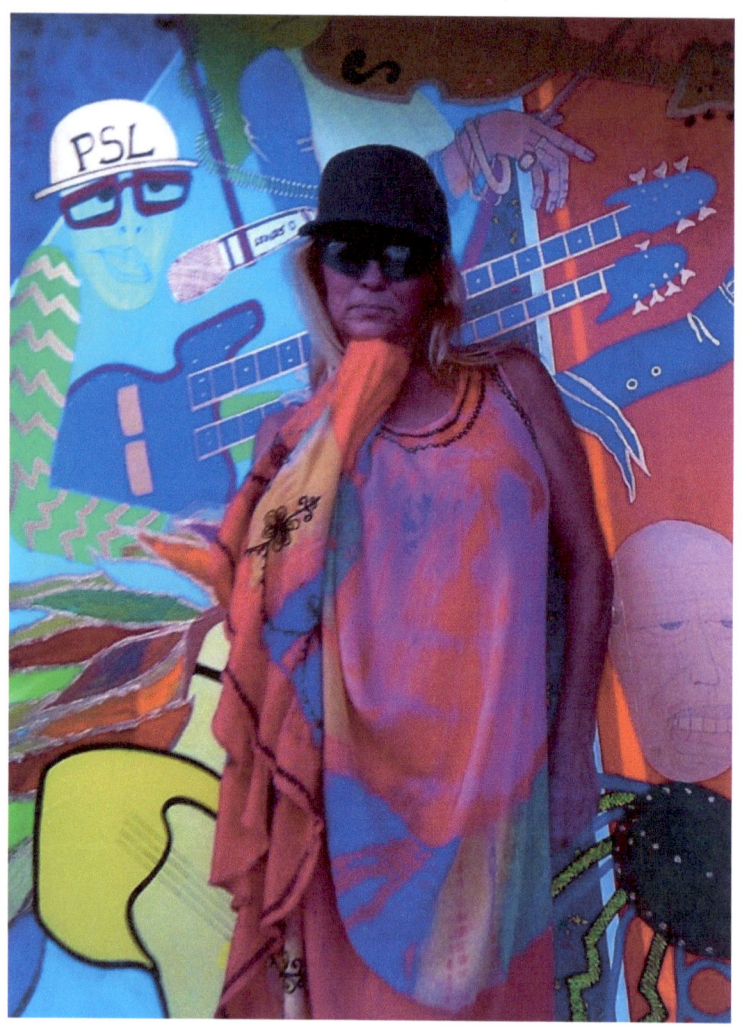

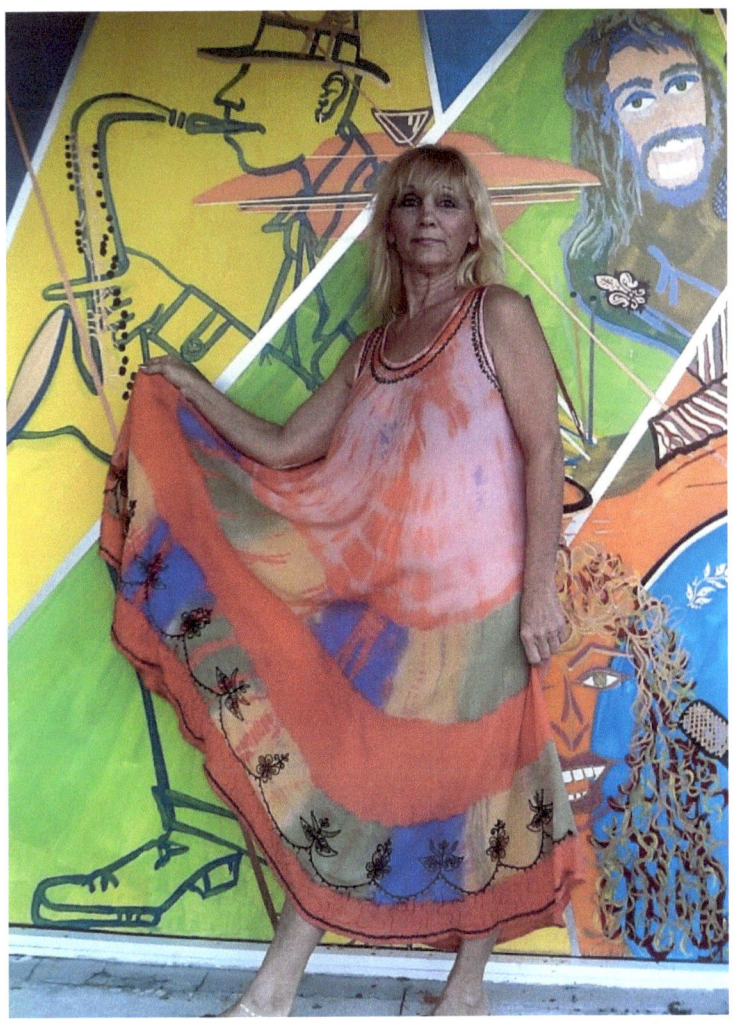

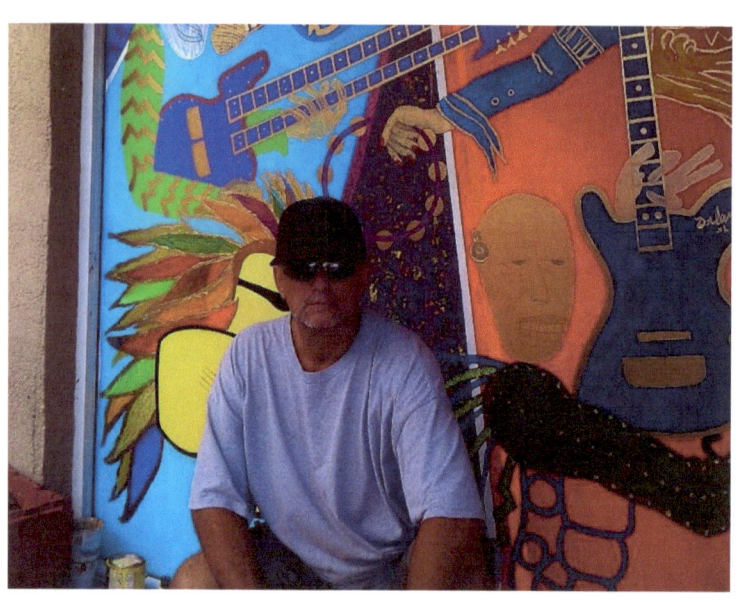

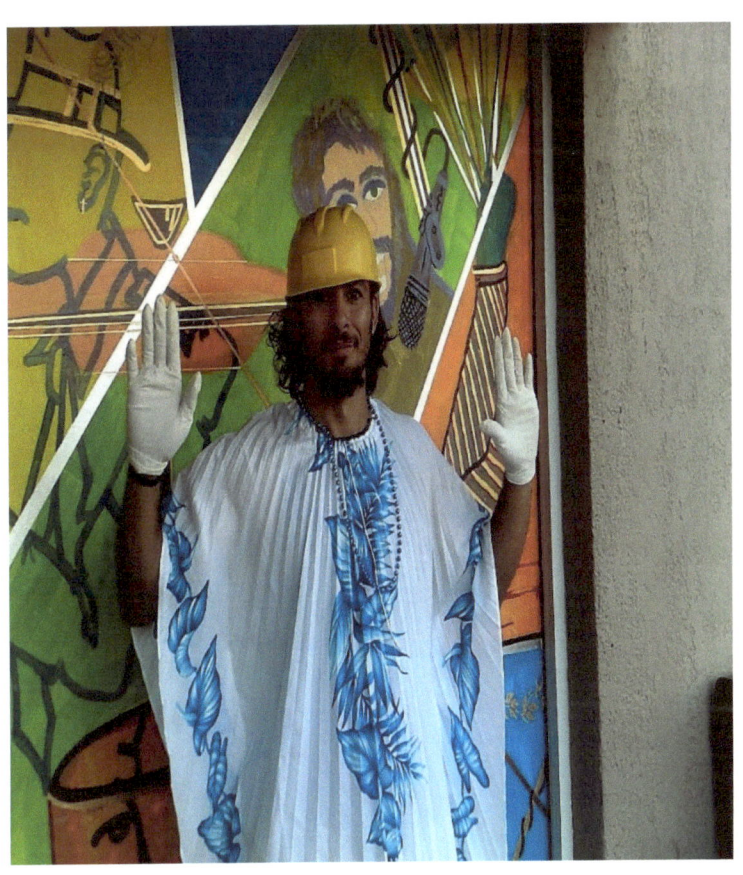

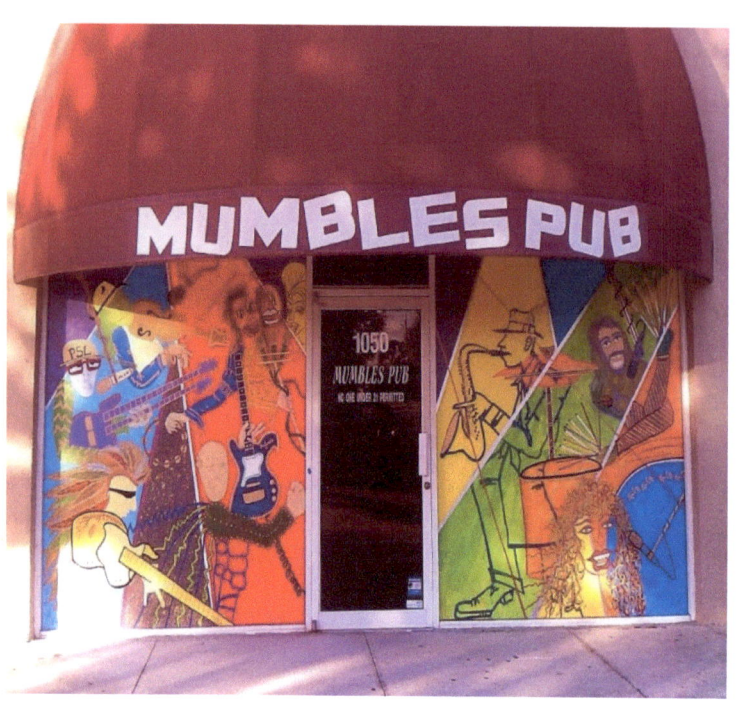

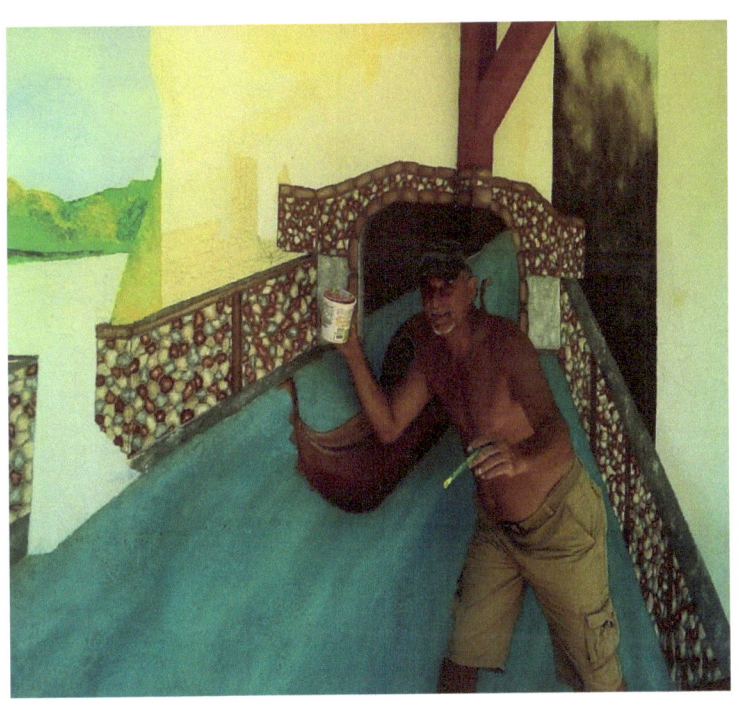

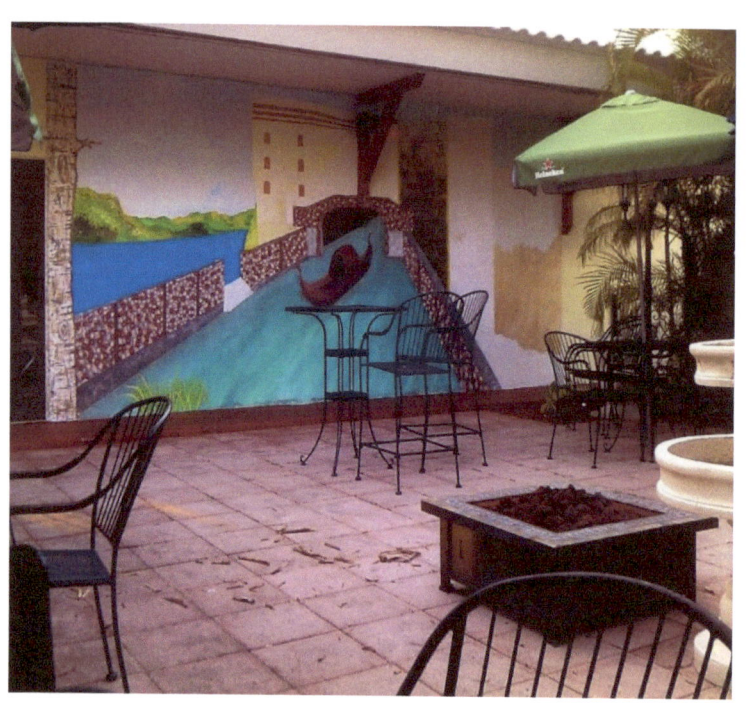

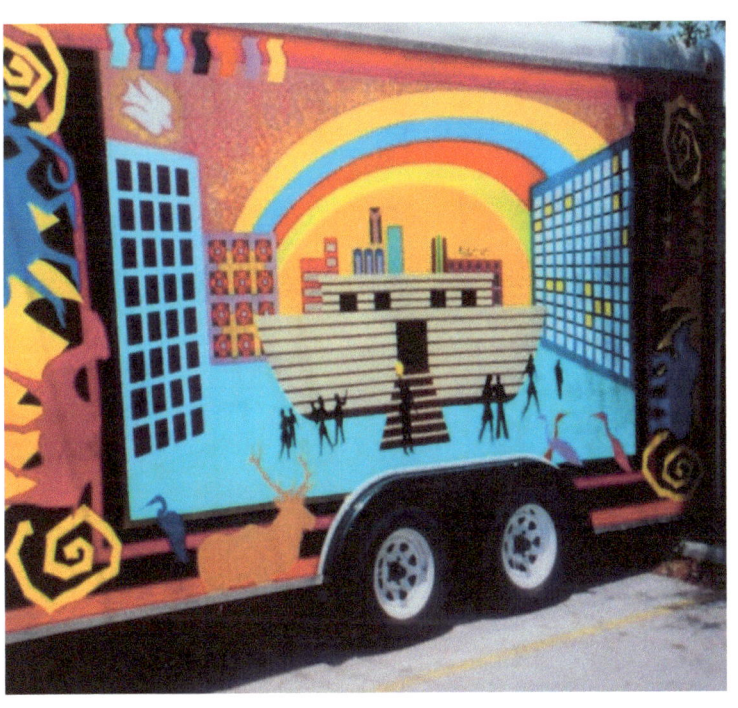

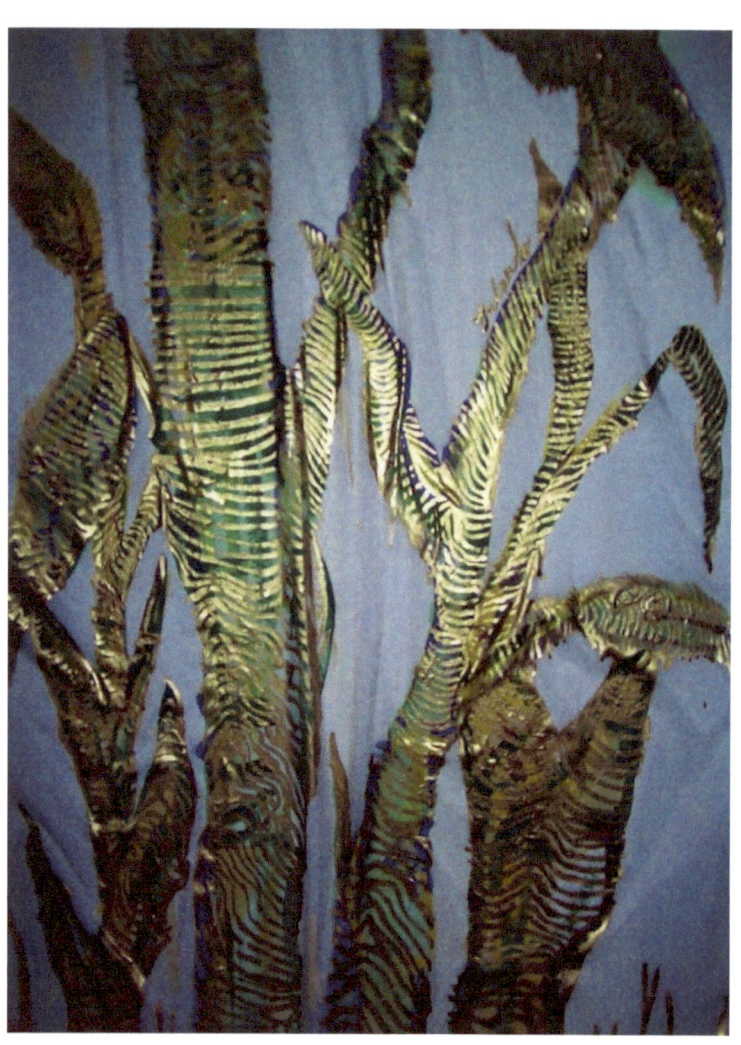

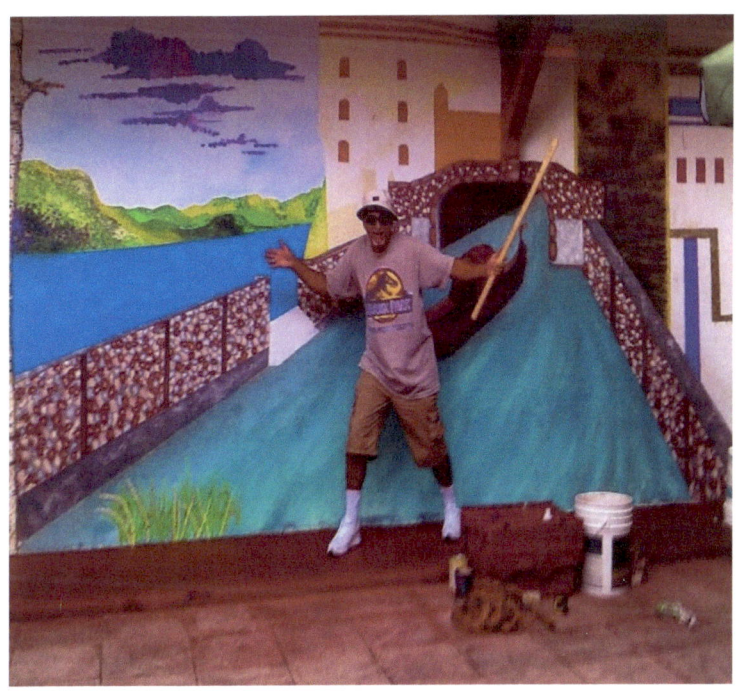

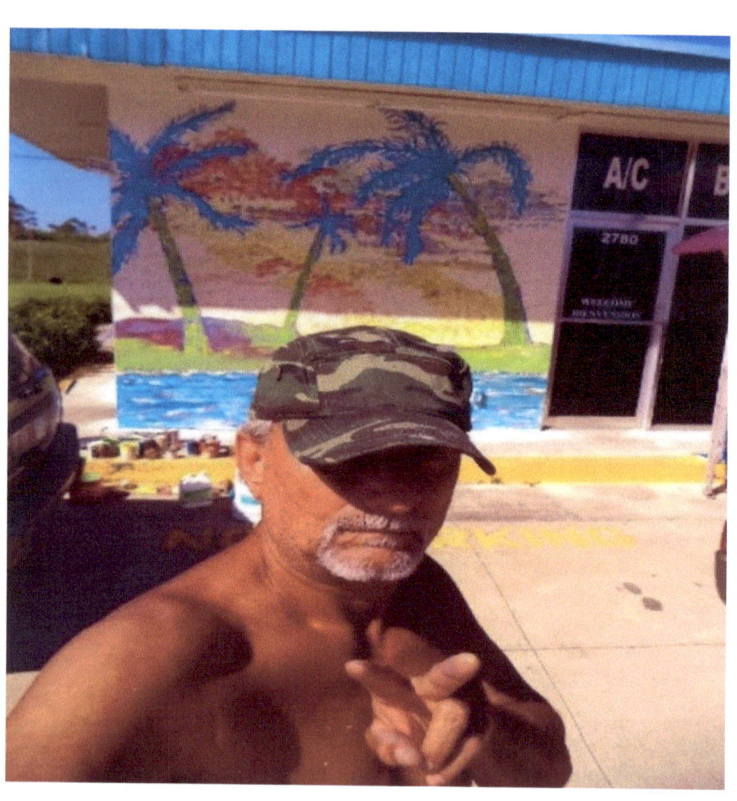

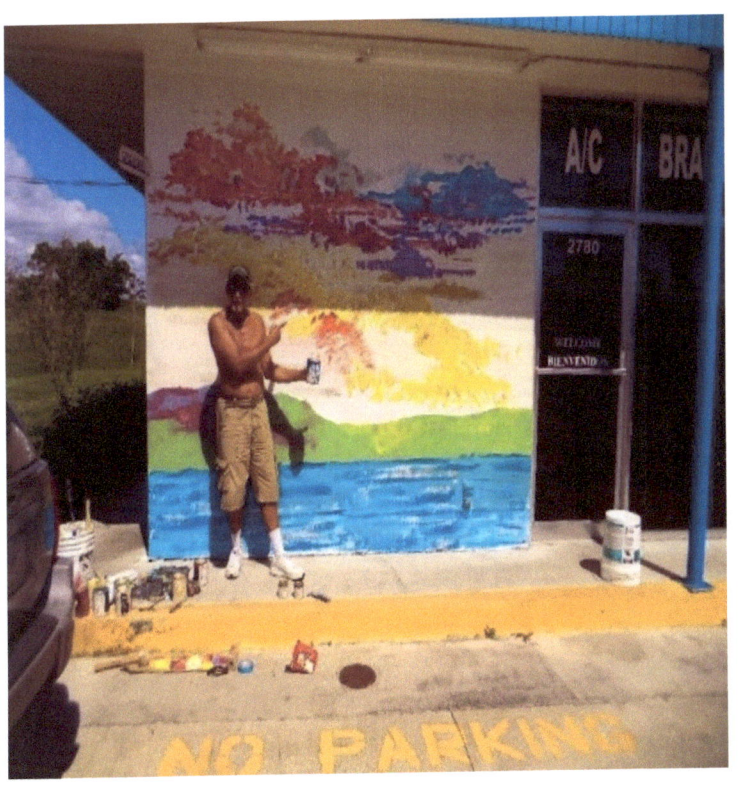

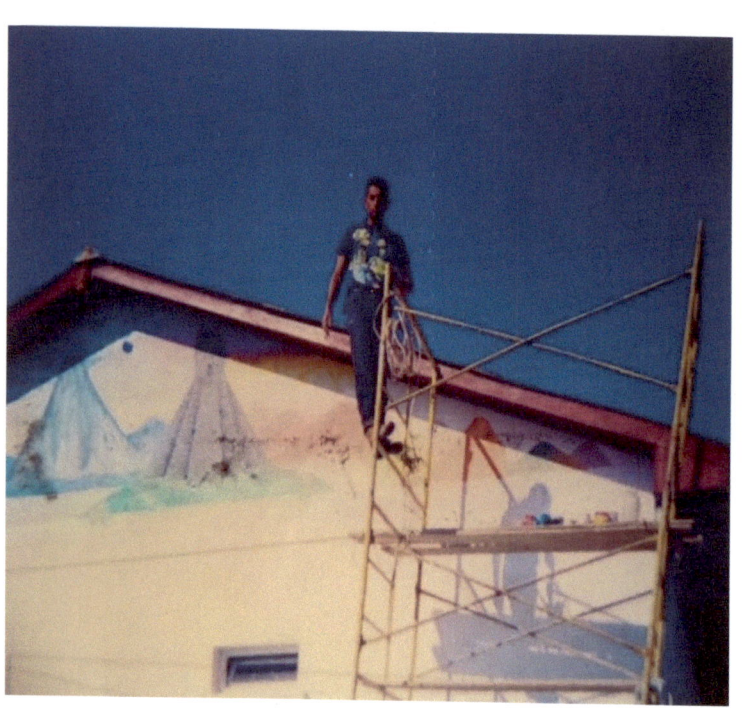

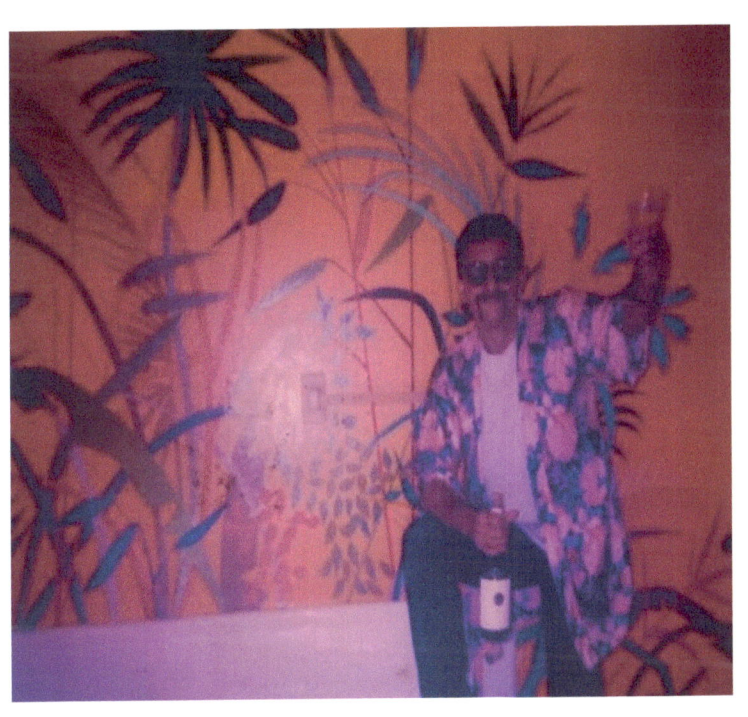

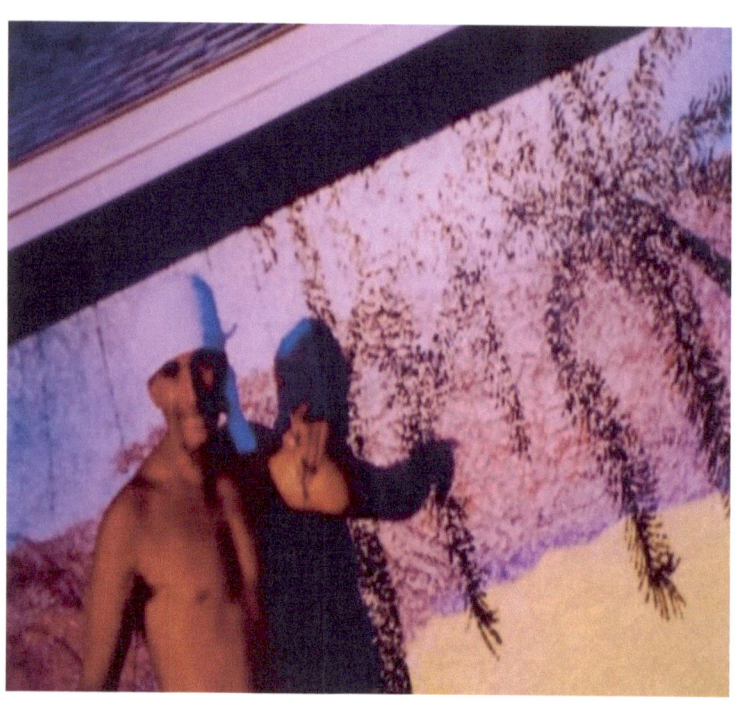

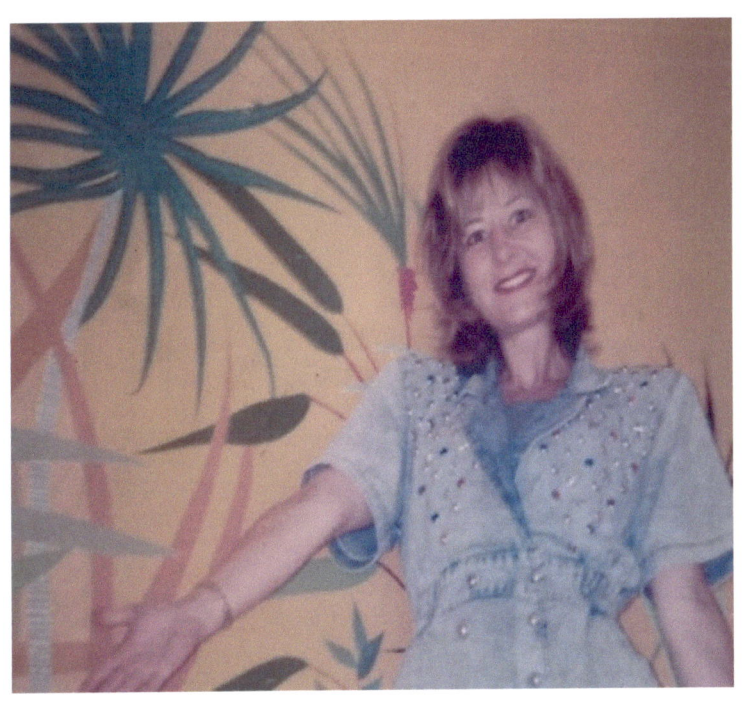

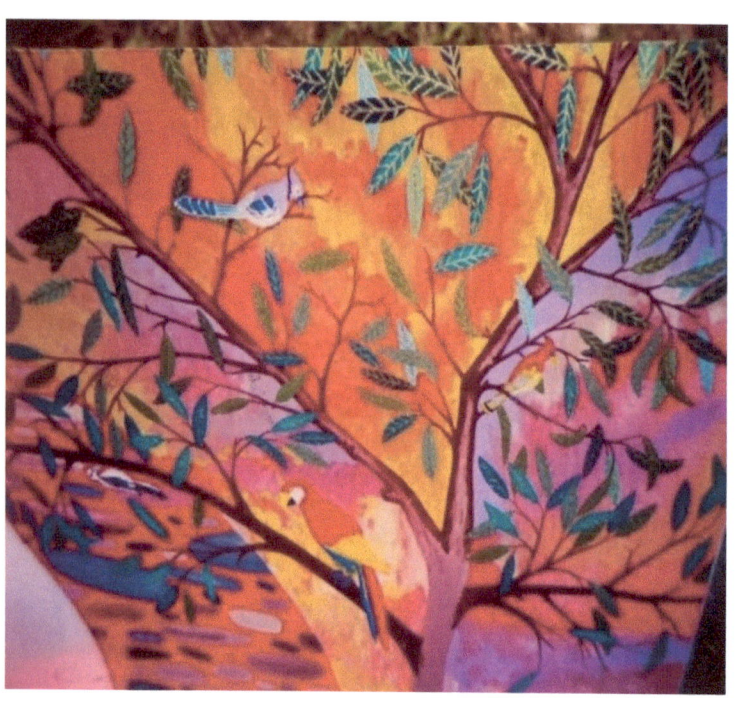

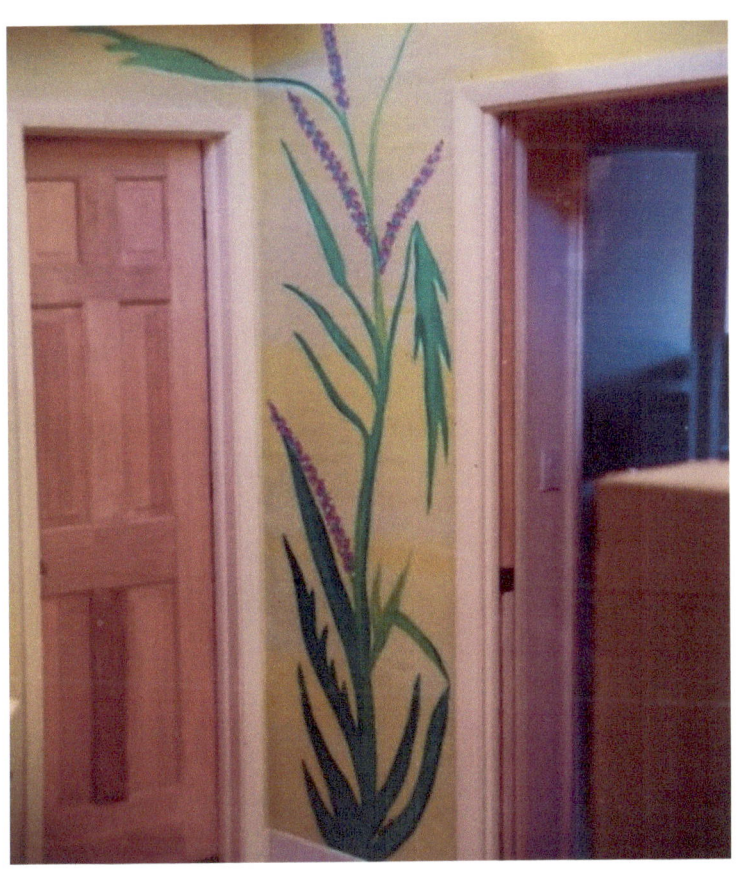

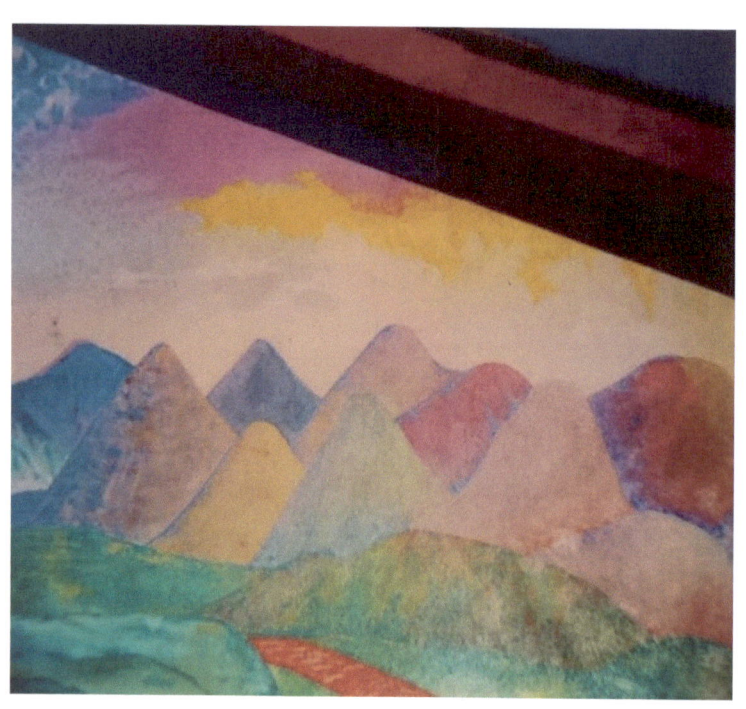

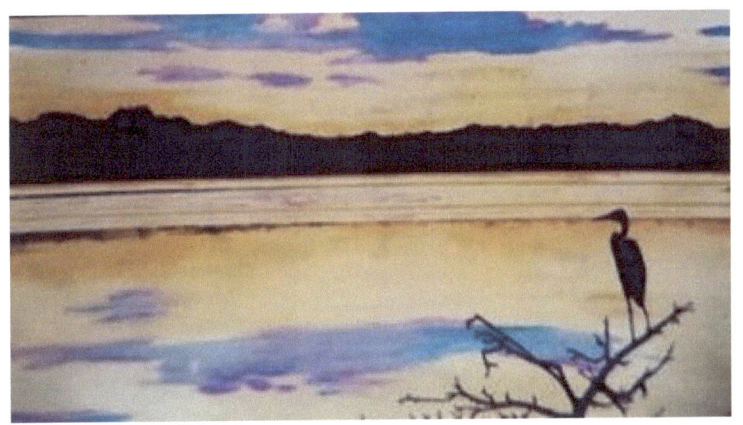

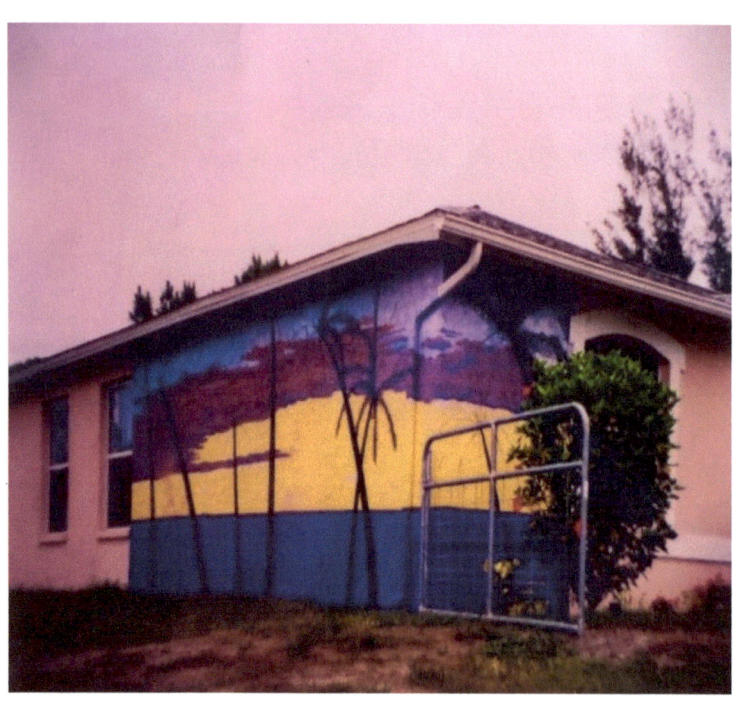

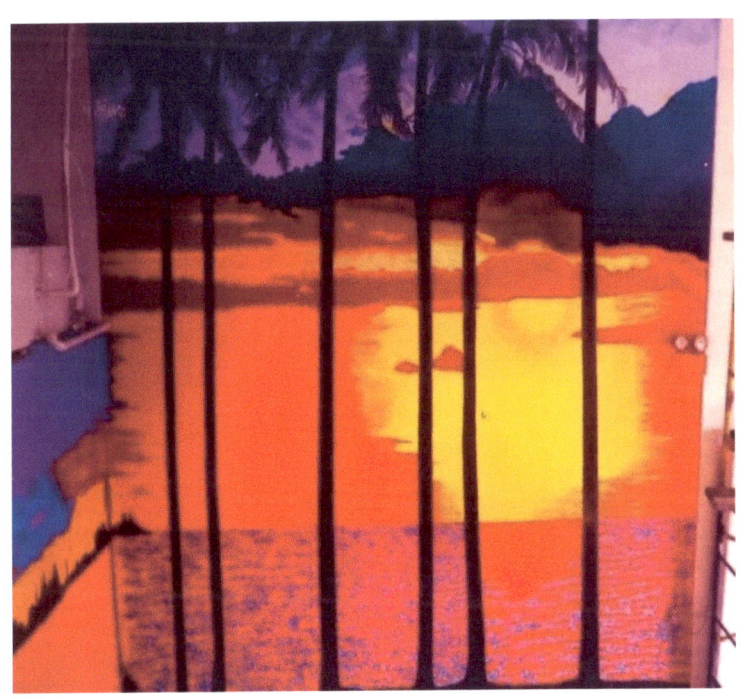

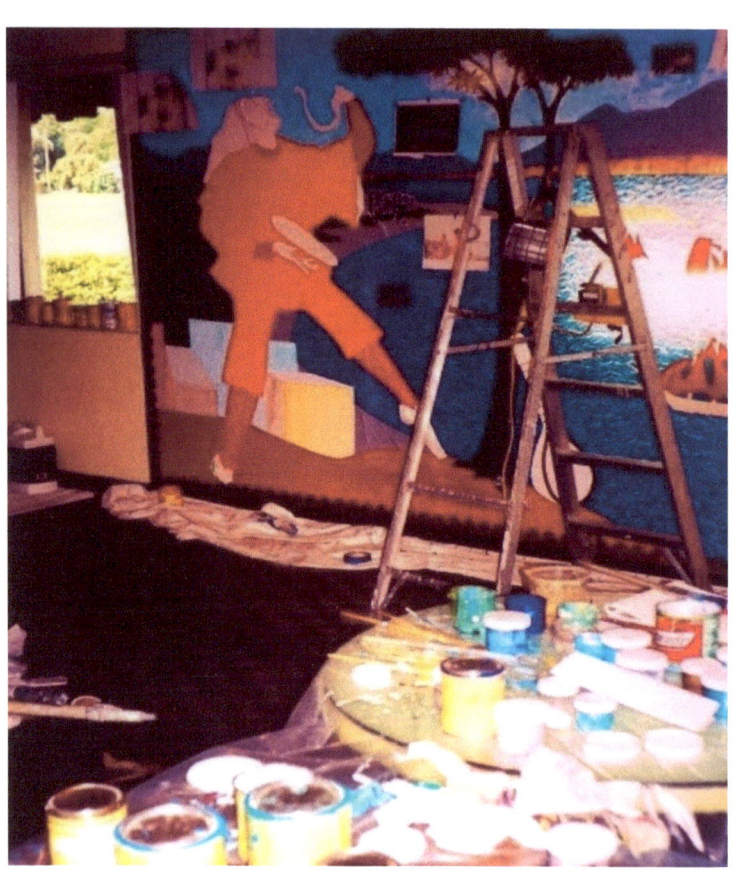

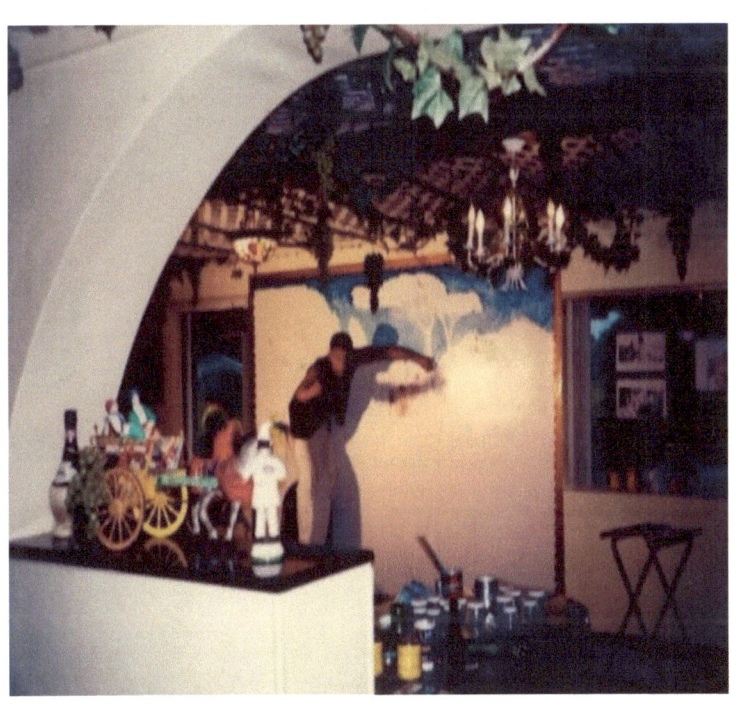

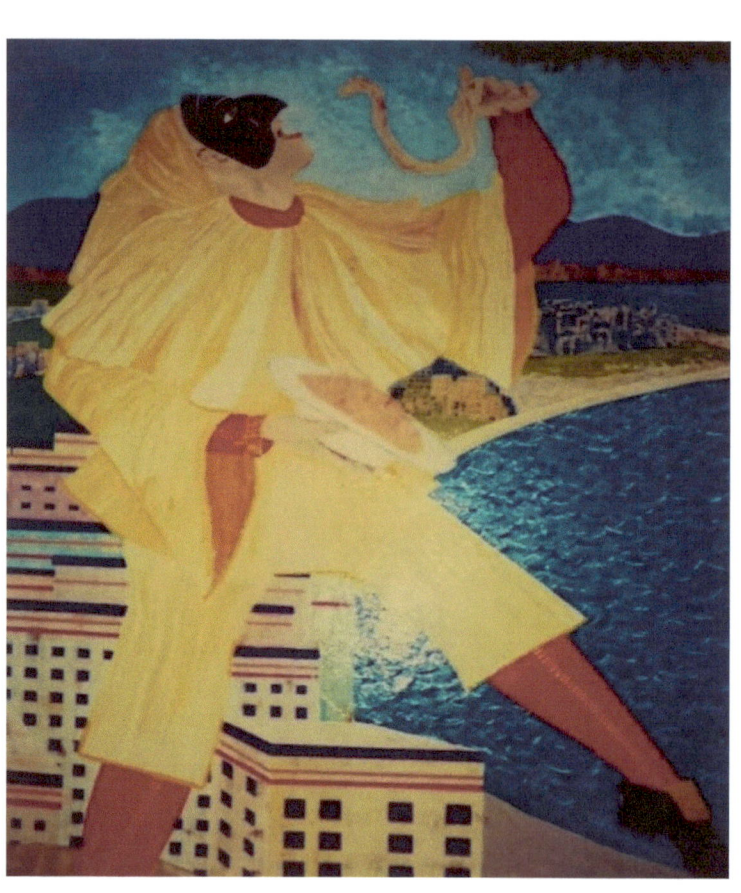

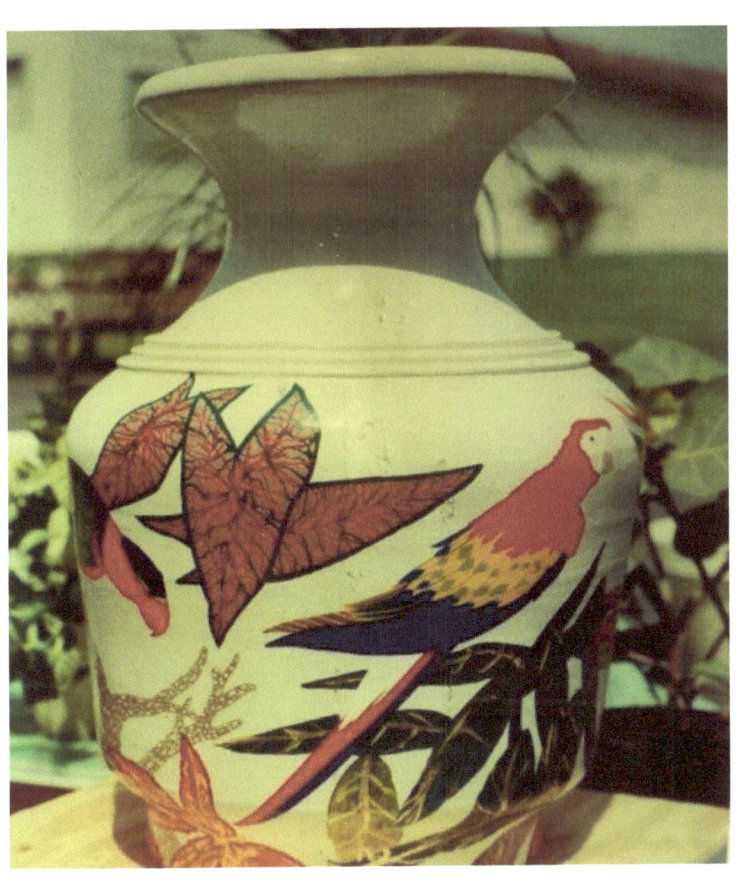

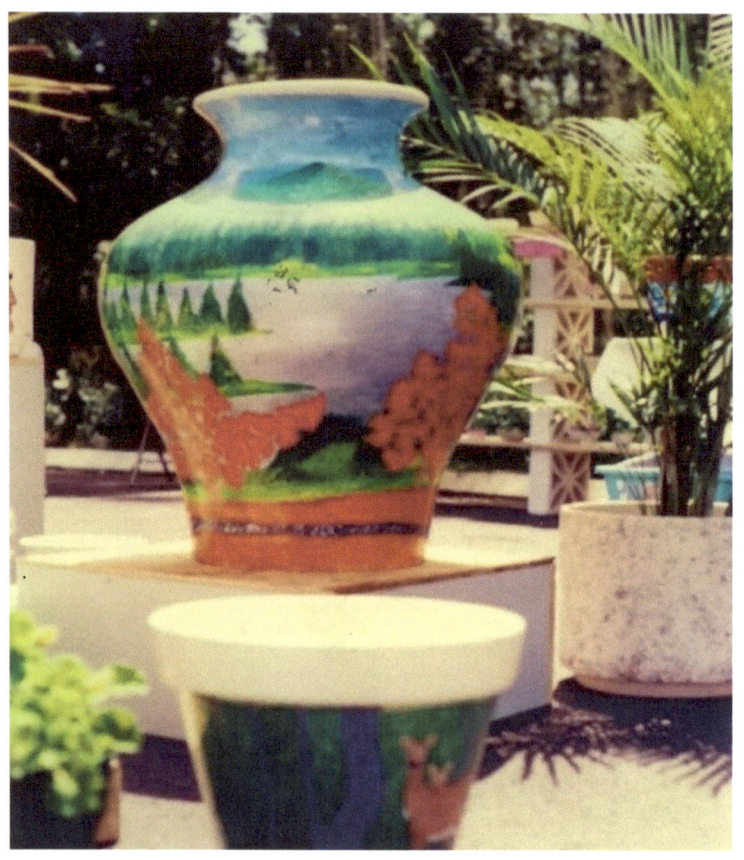

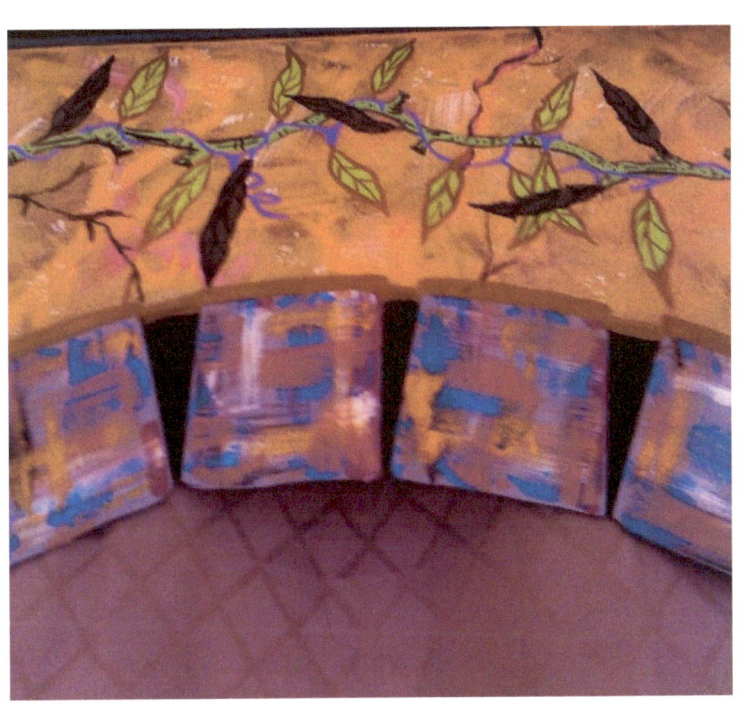

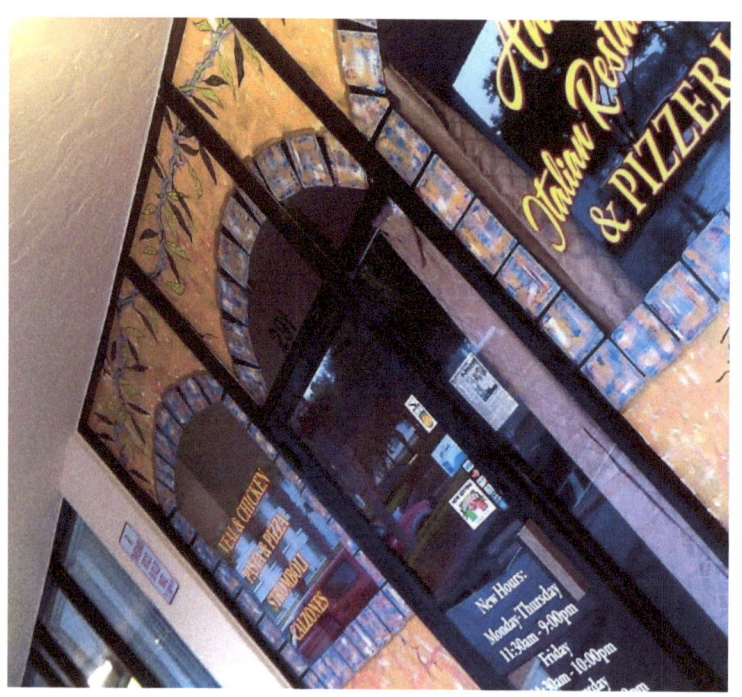

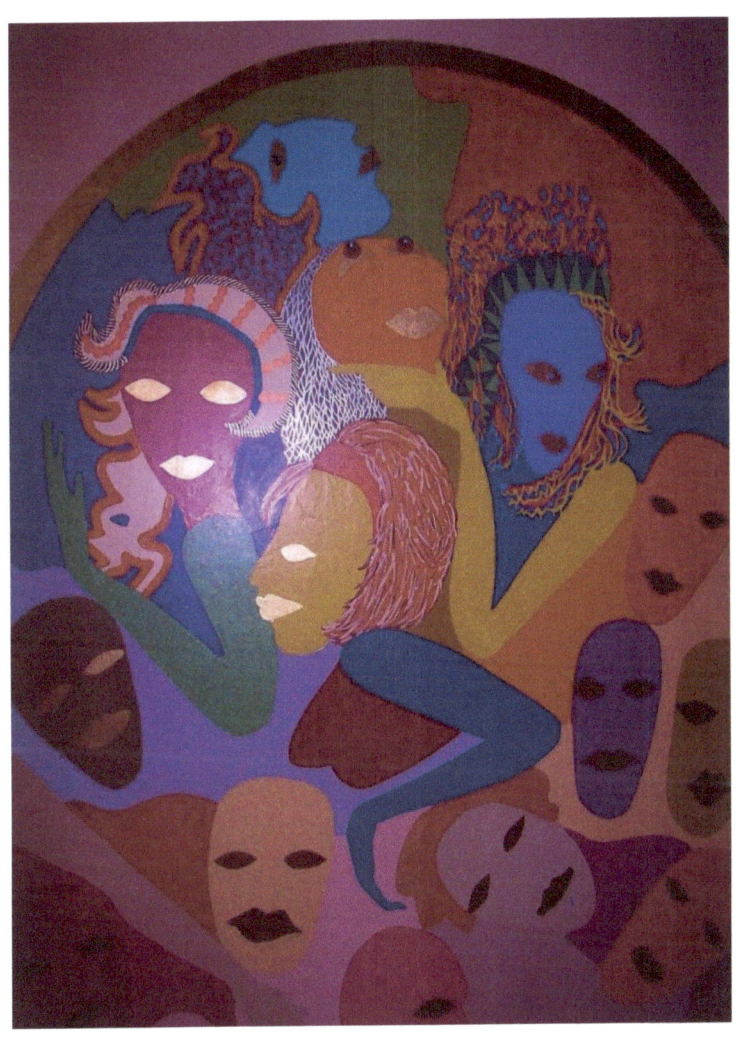

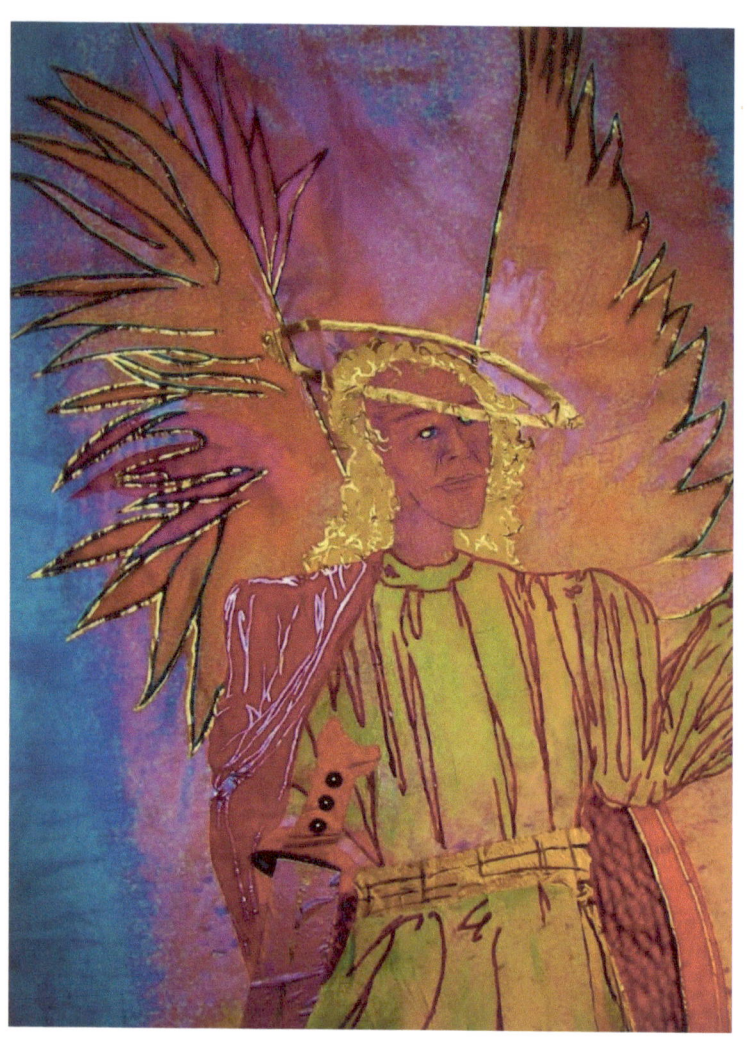

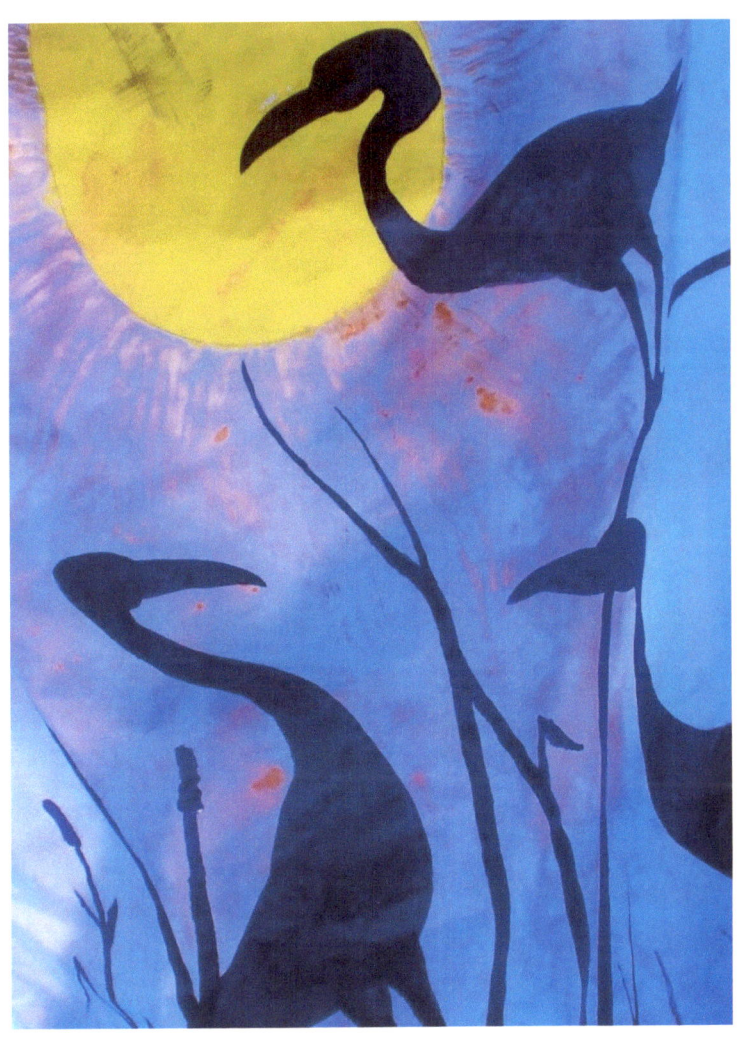

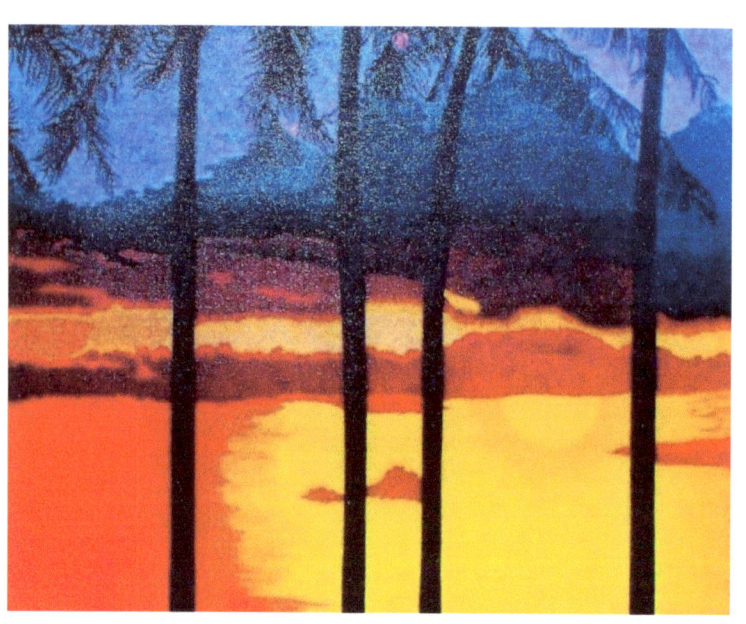

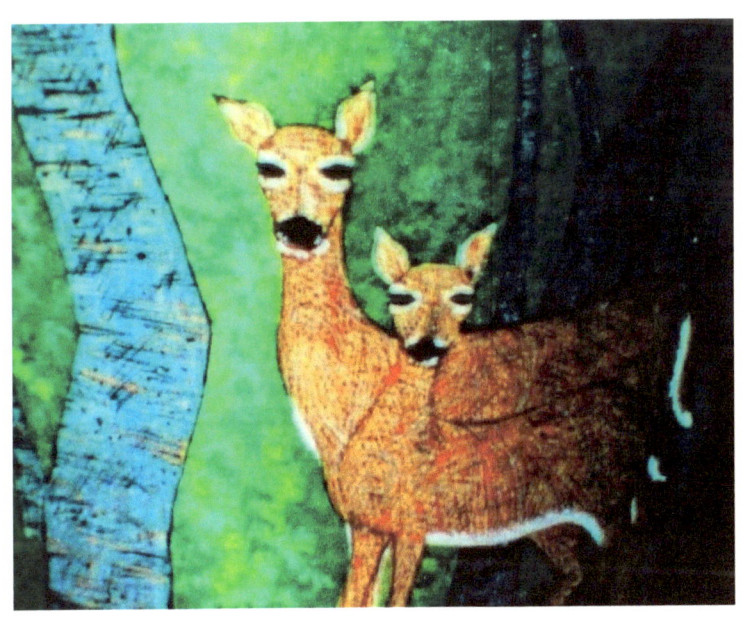

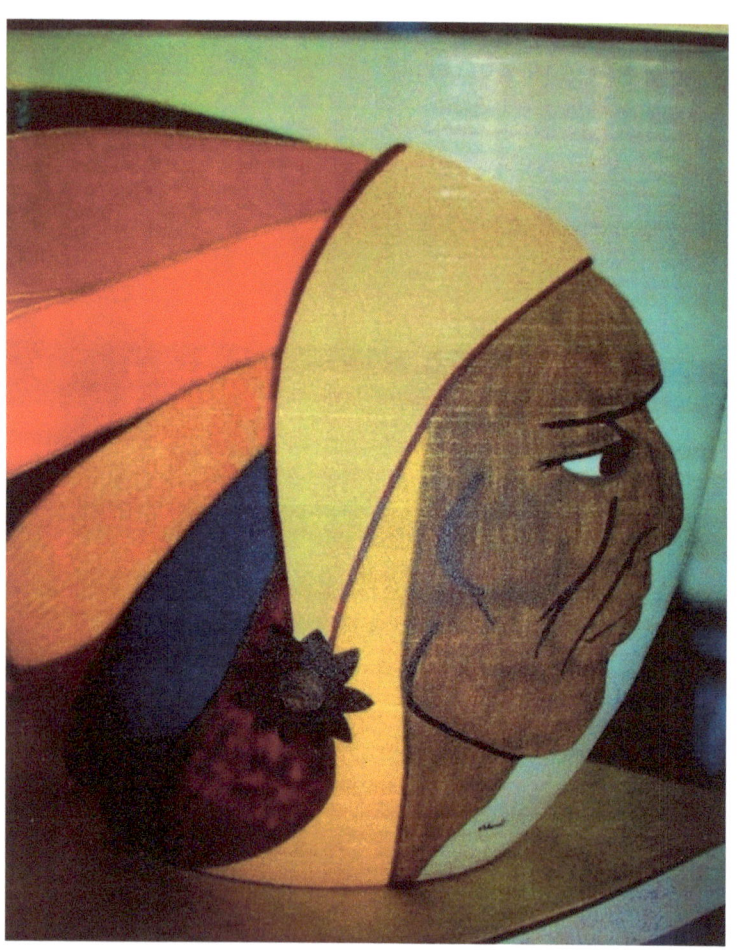

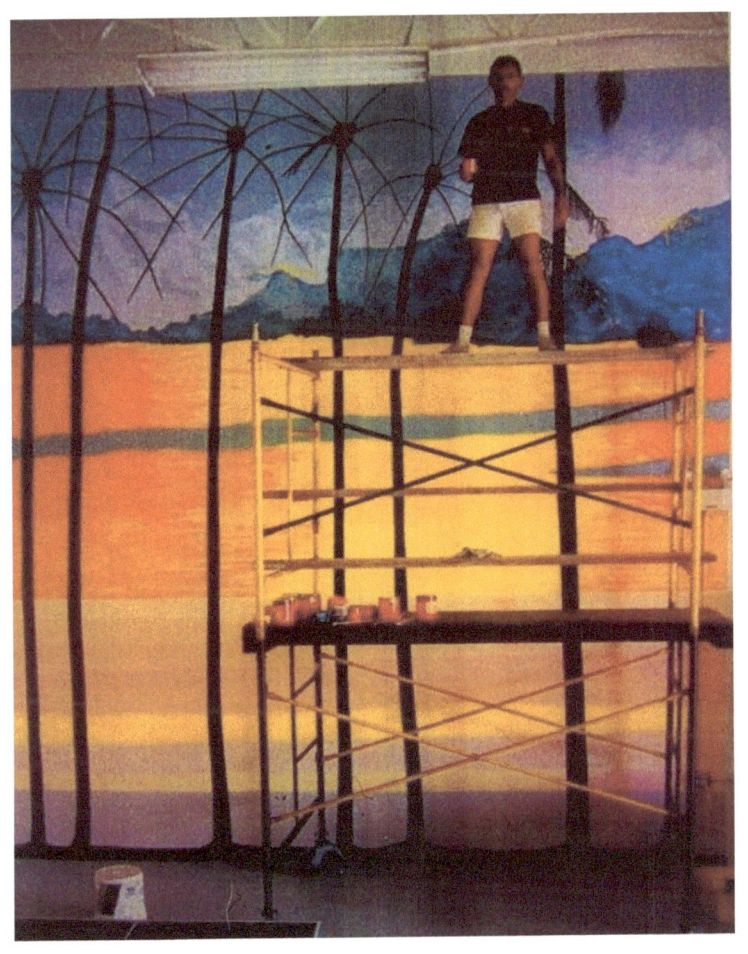

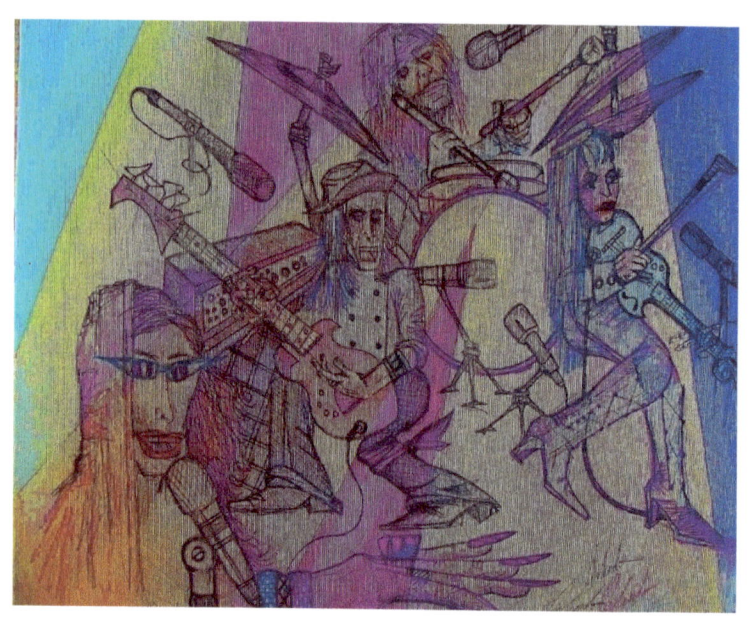

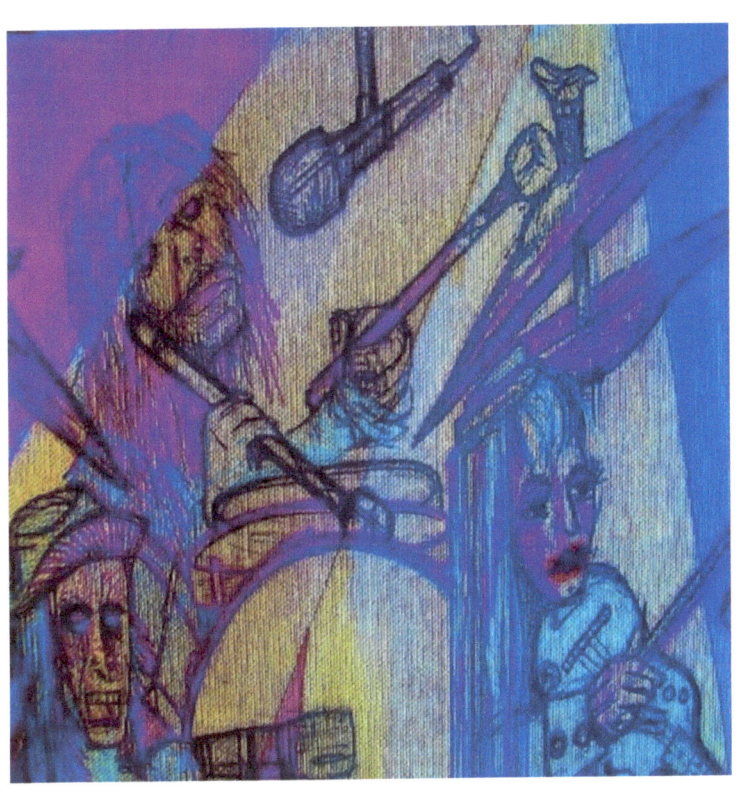

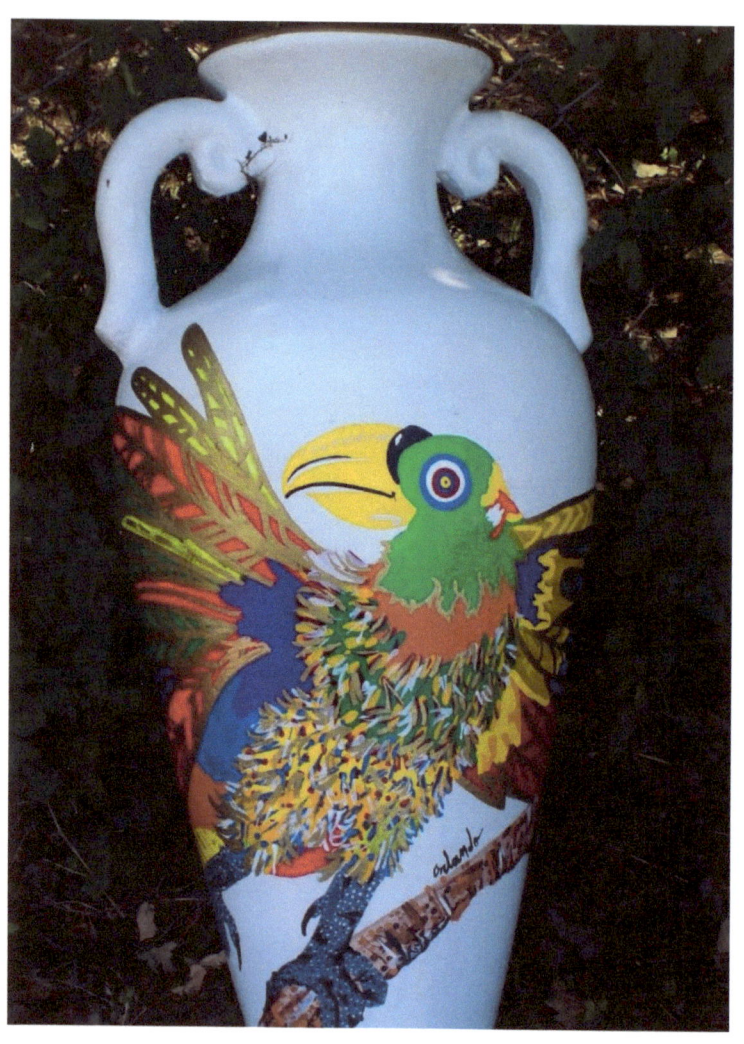

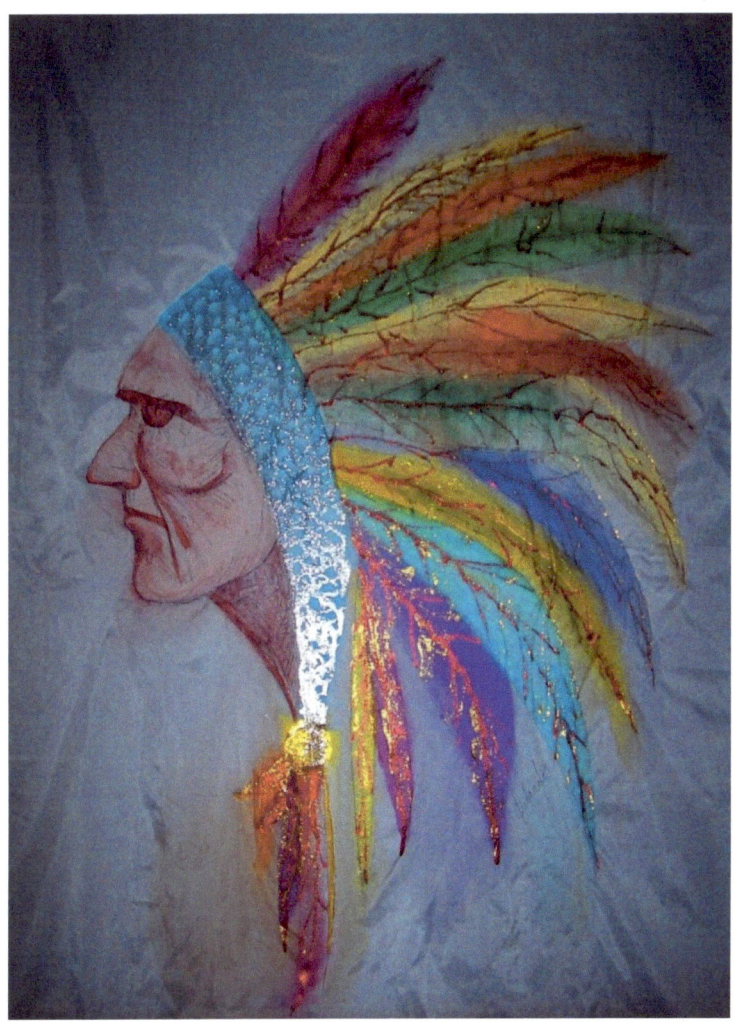

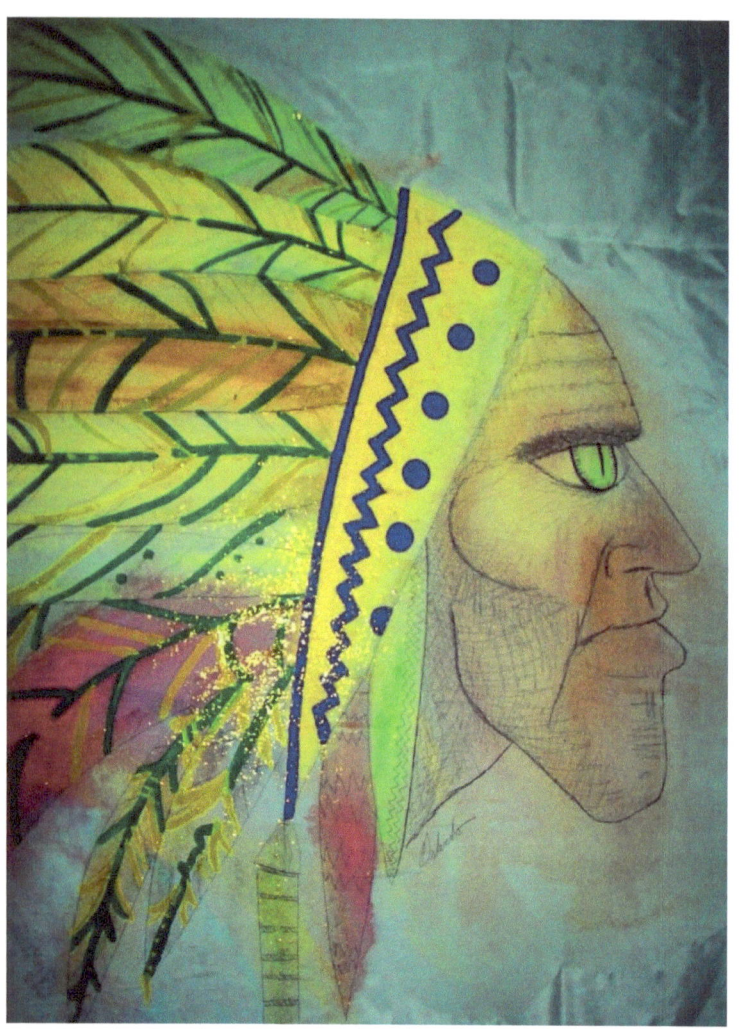

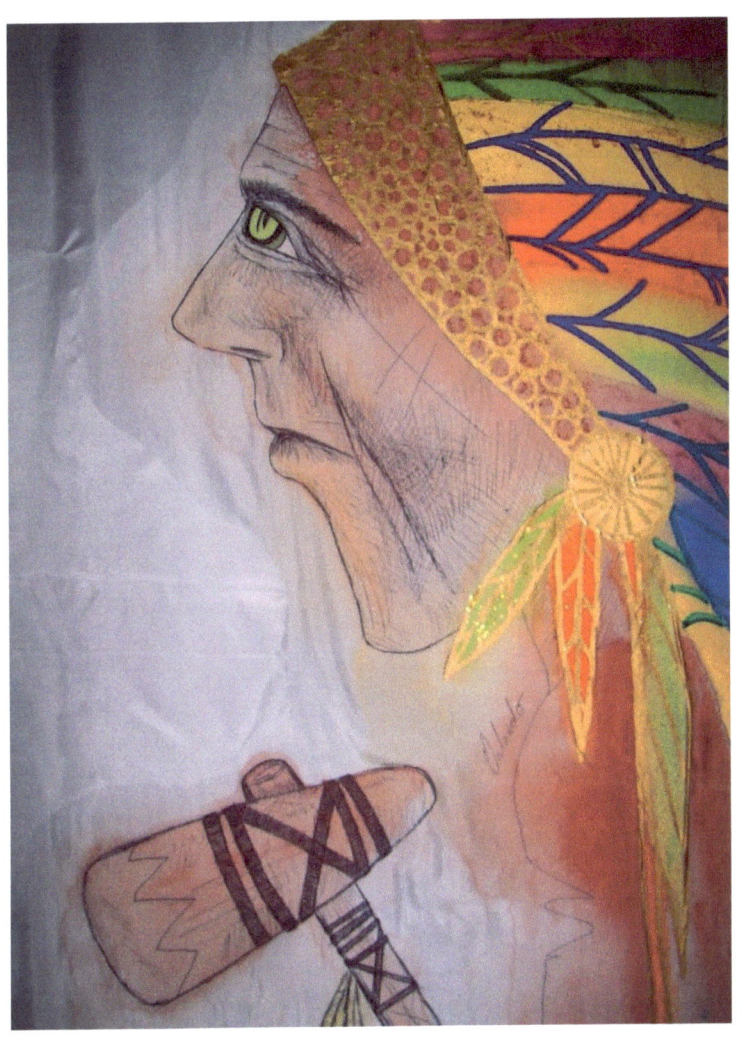

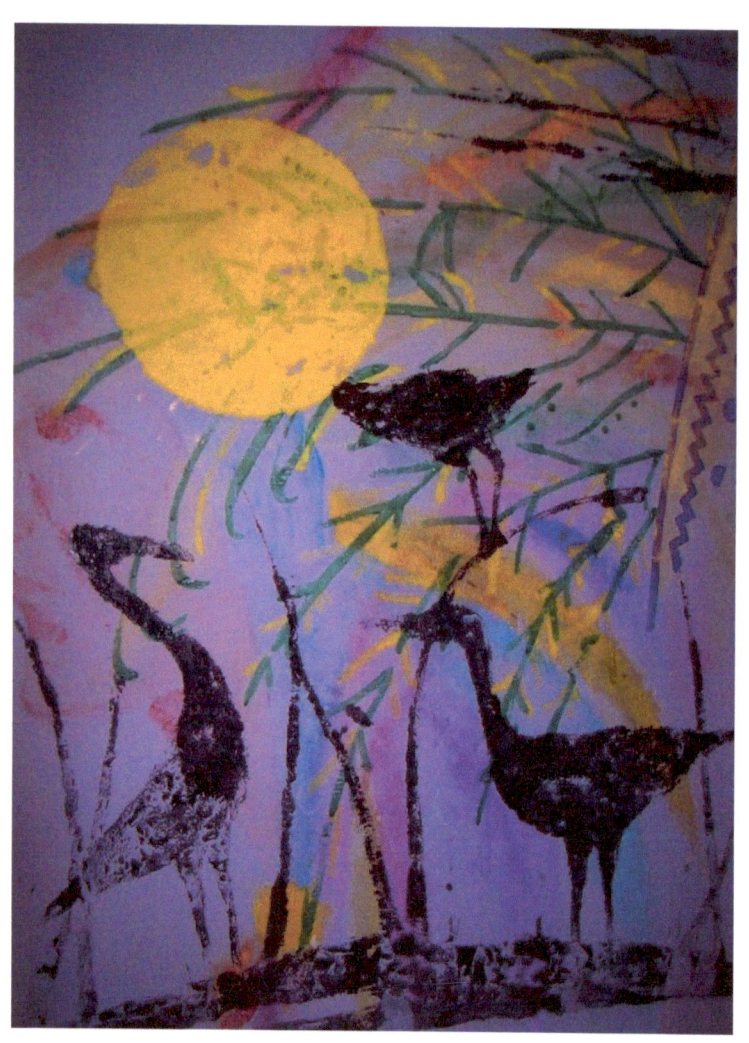

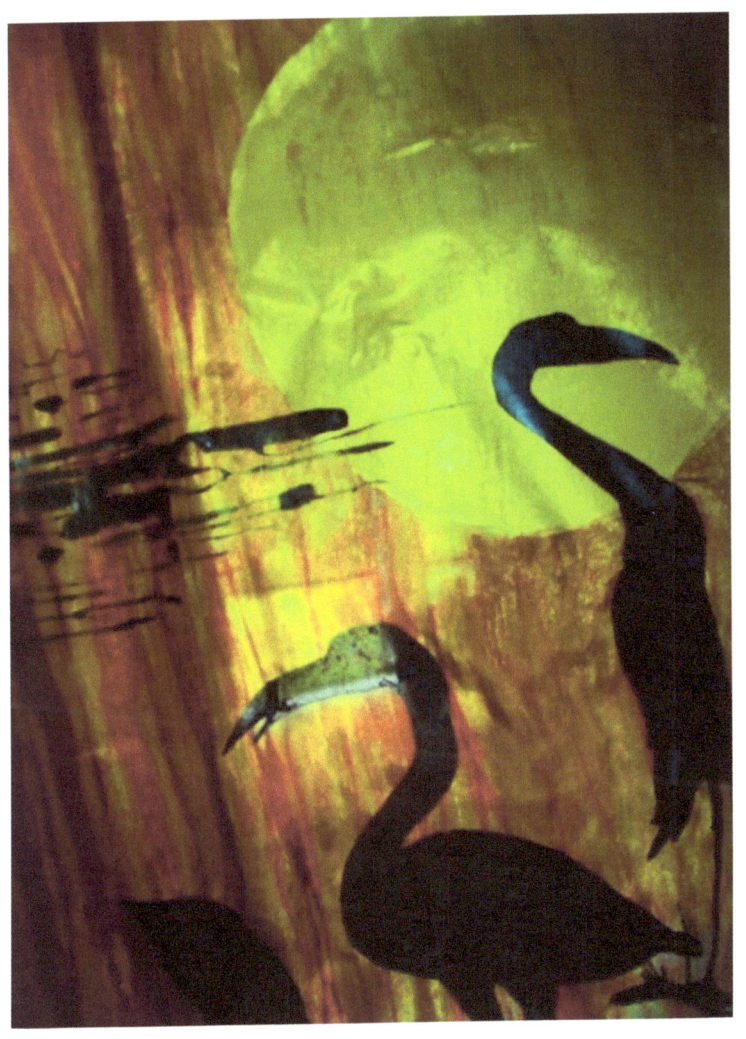

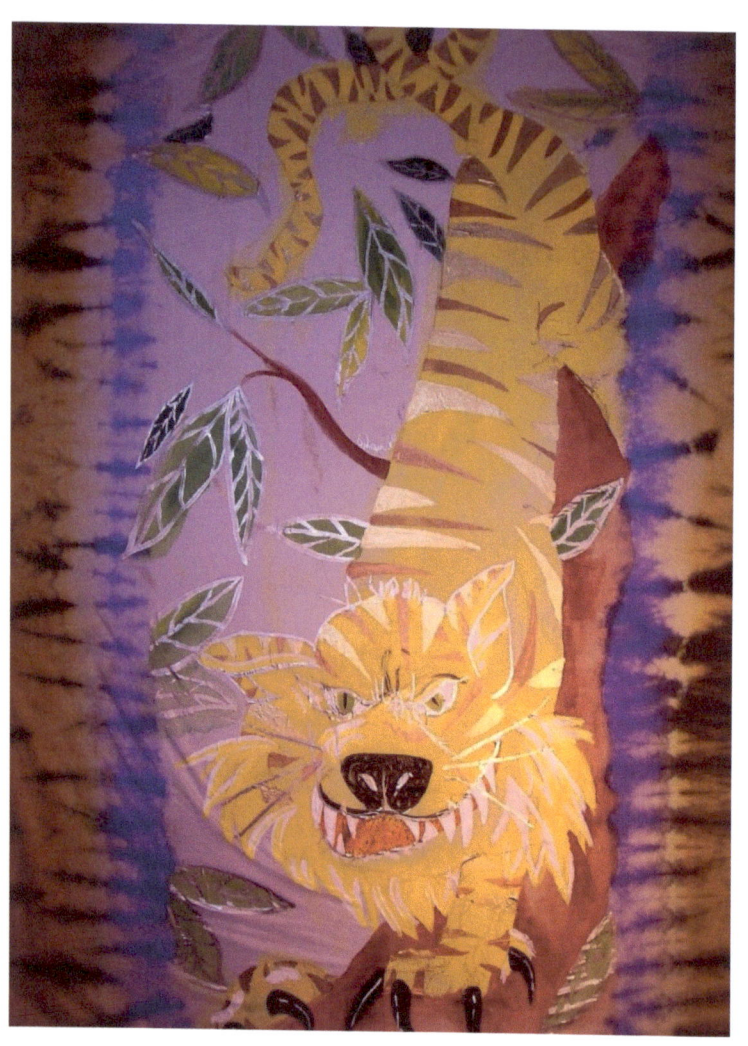

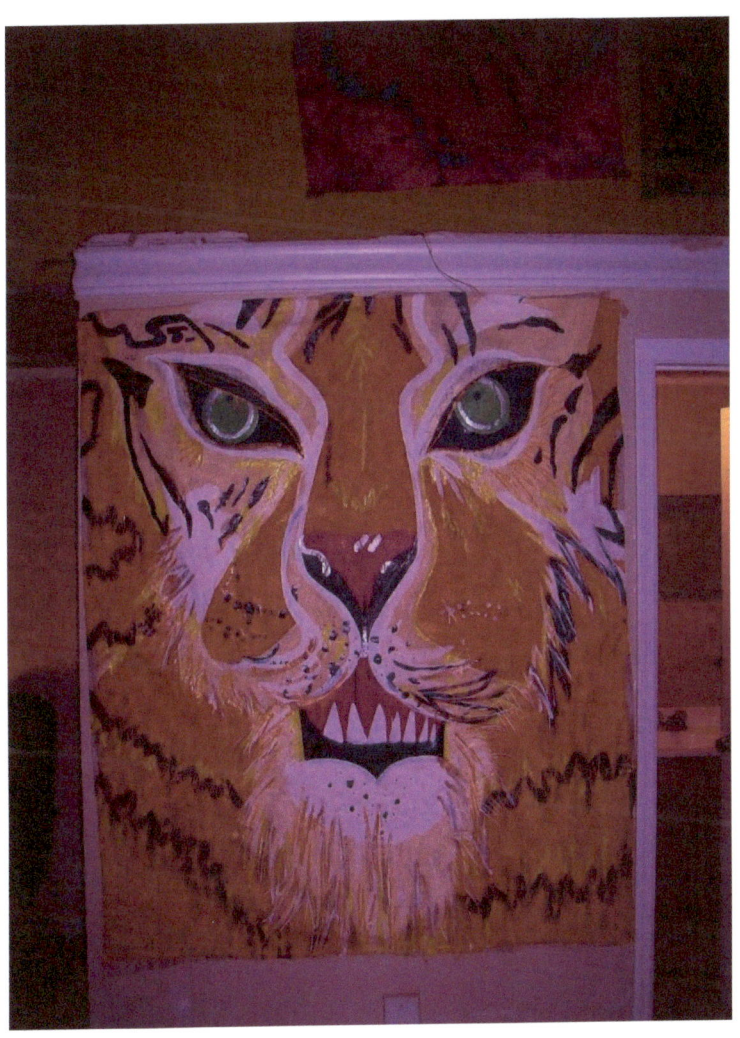

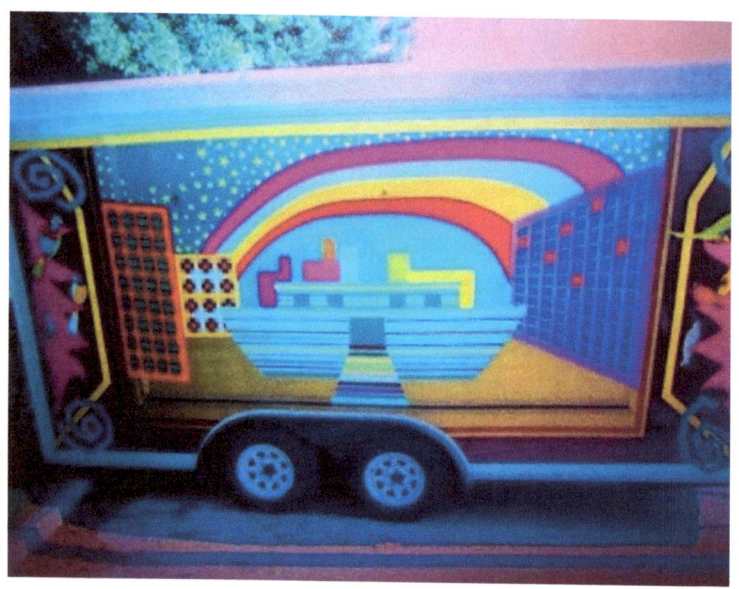

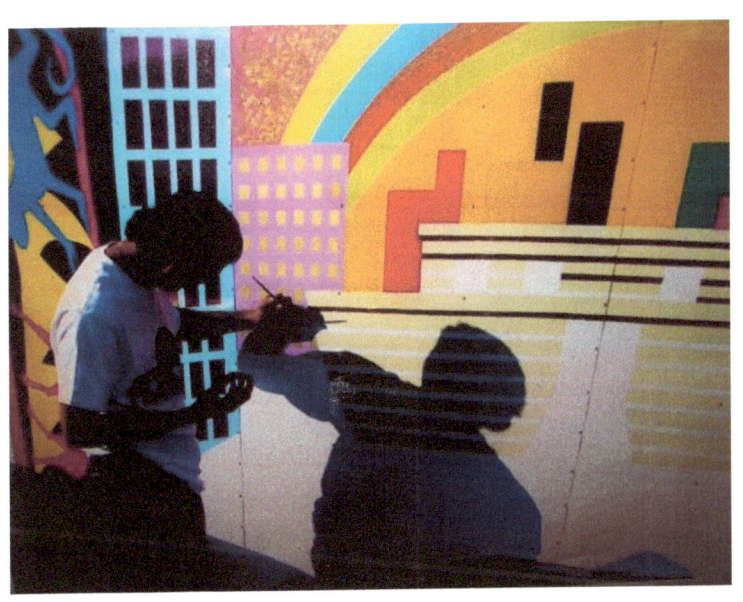

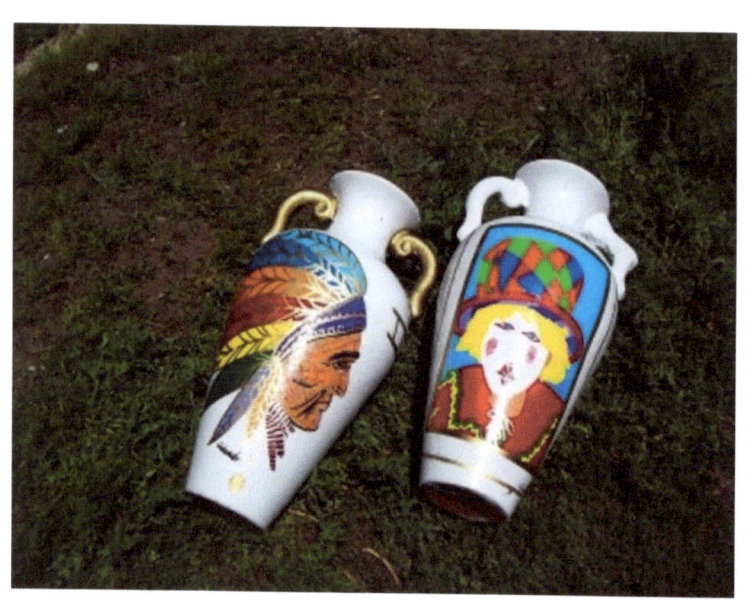

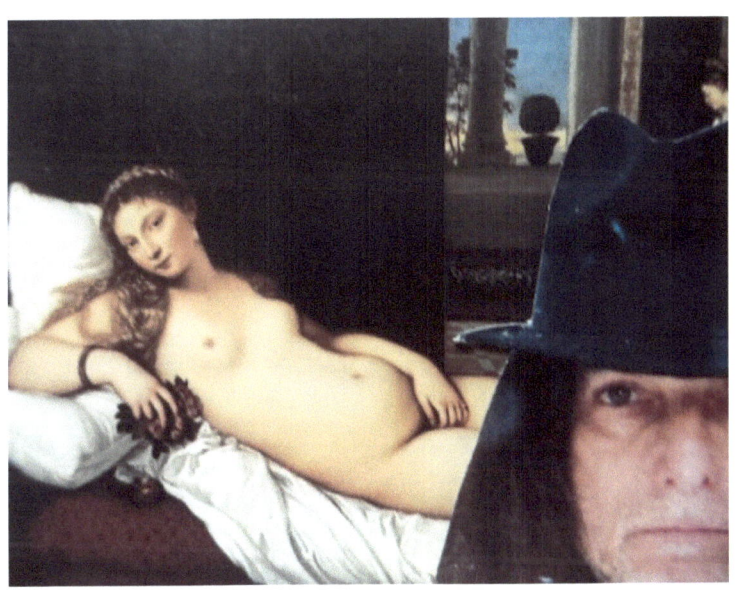

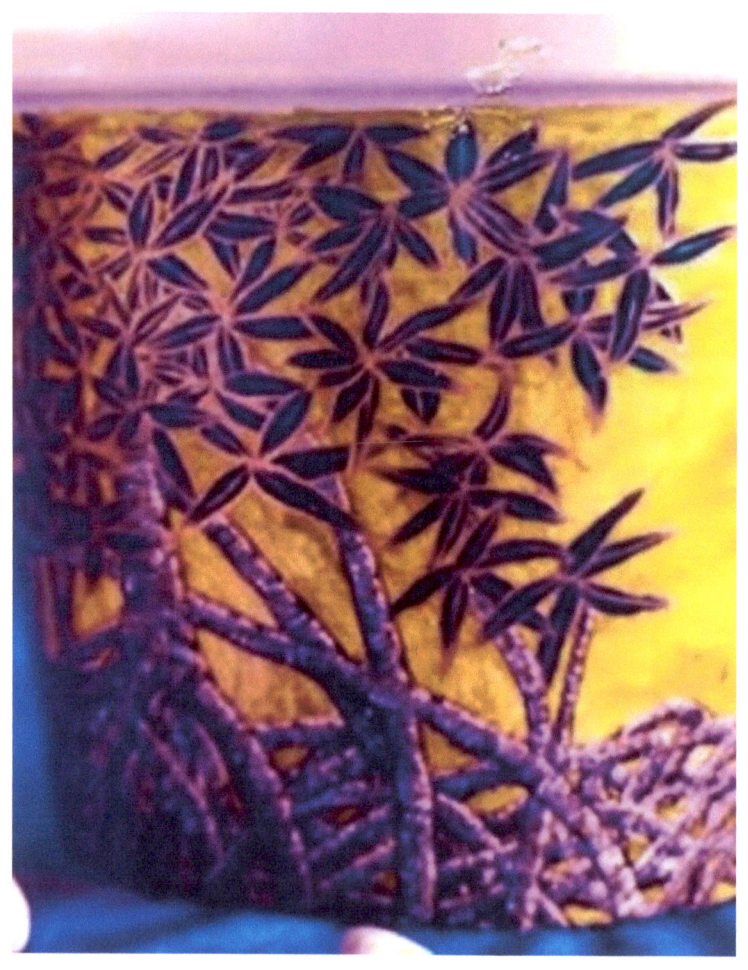

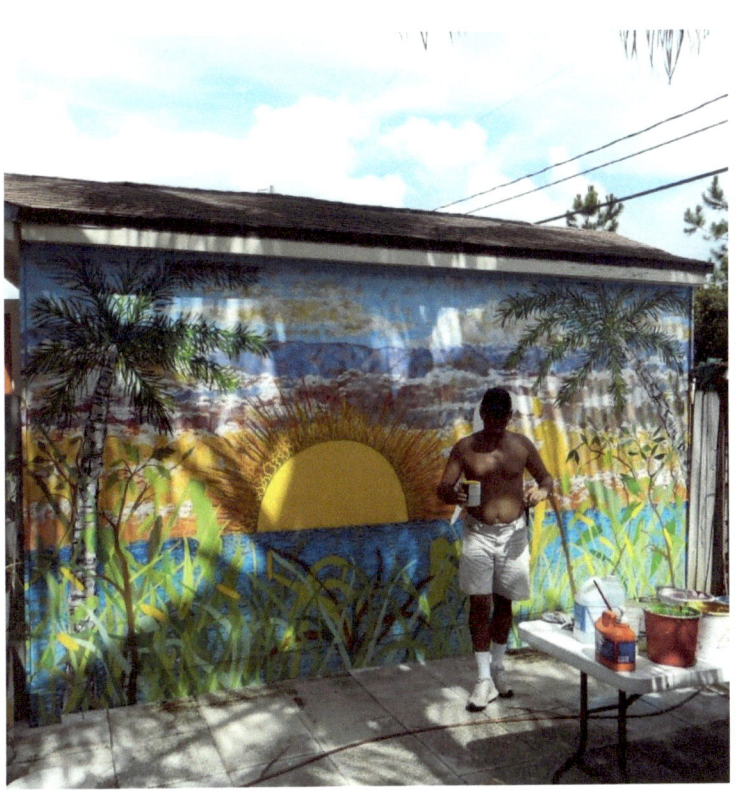

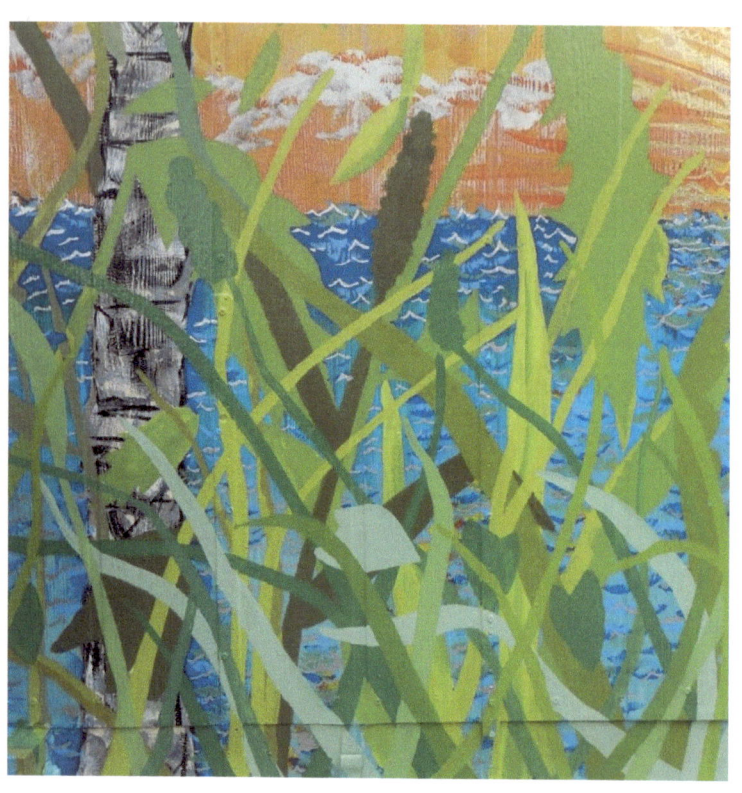

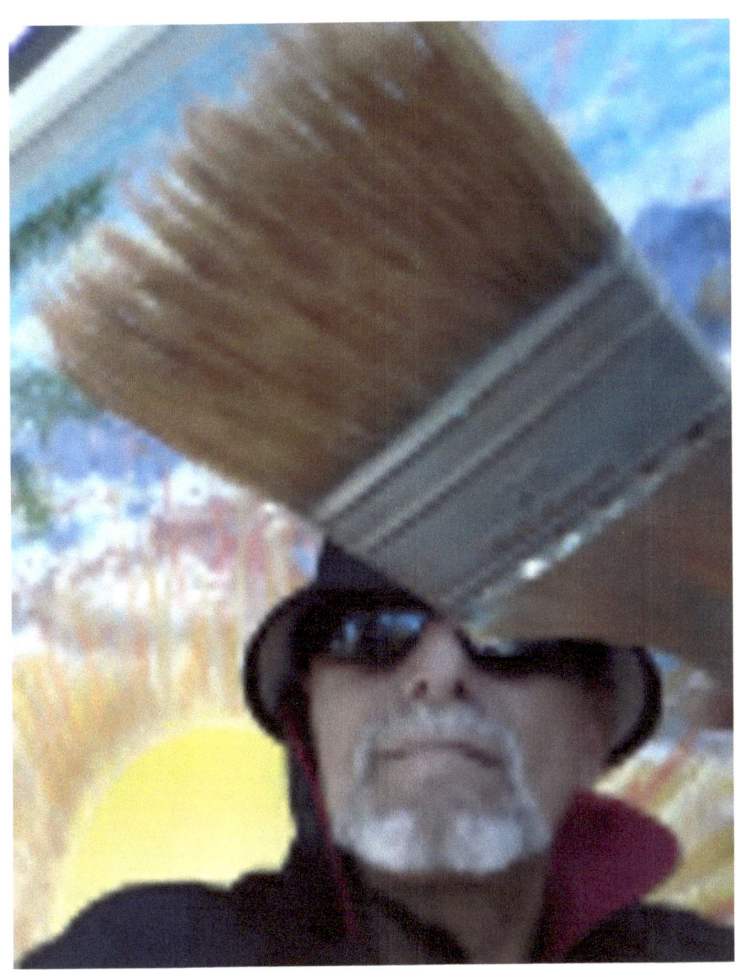

63

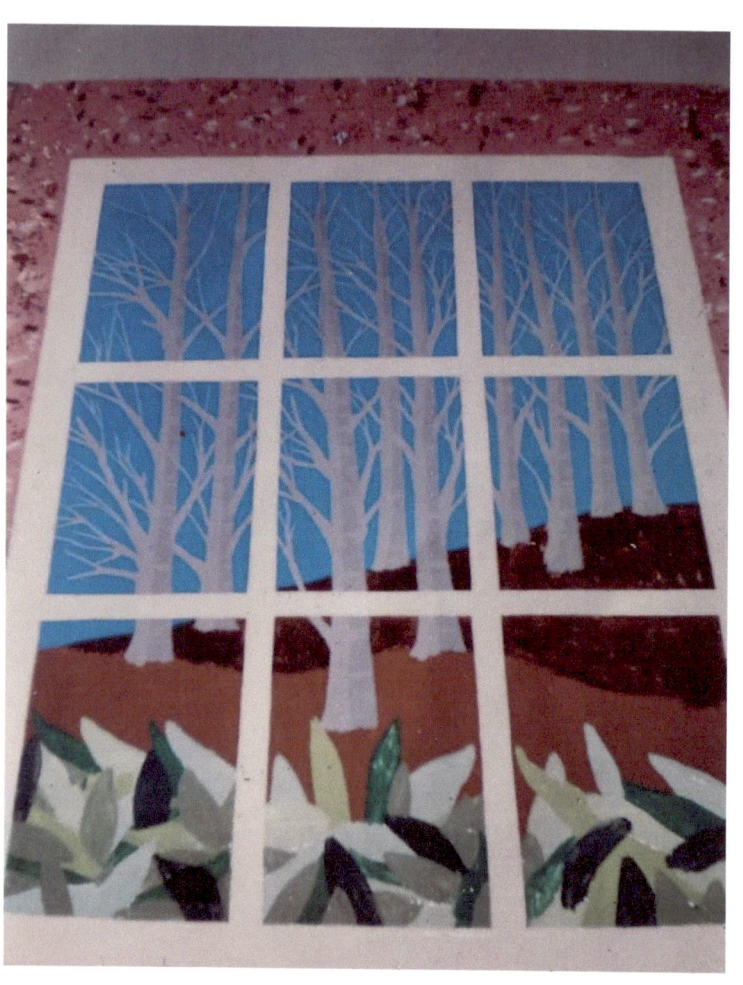

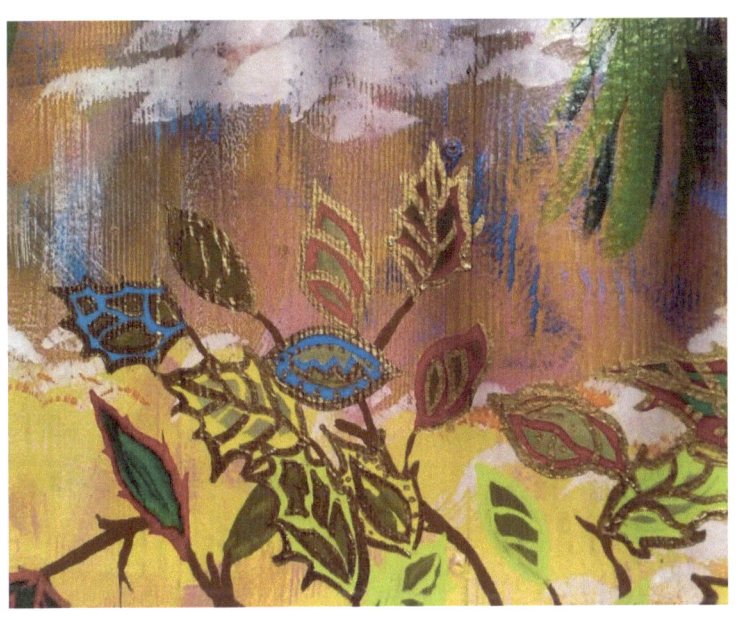

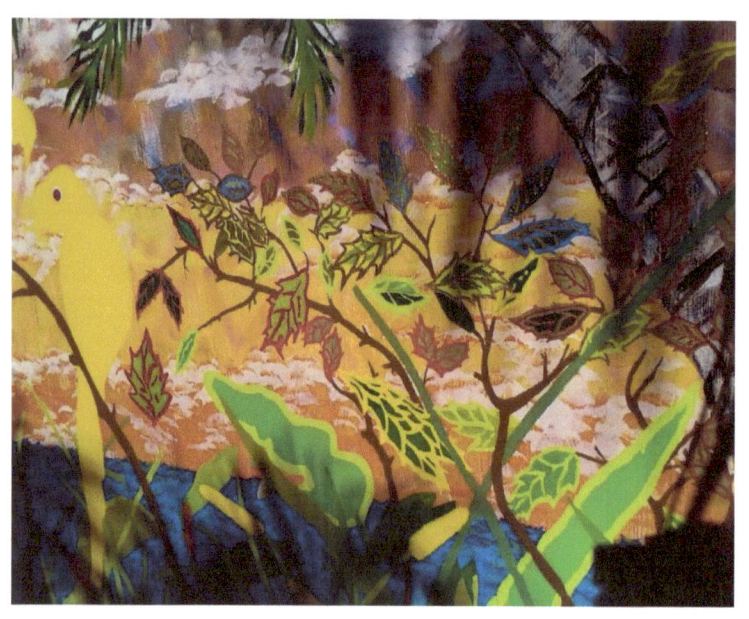

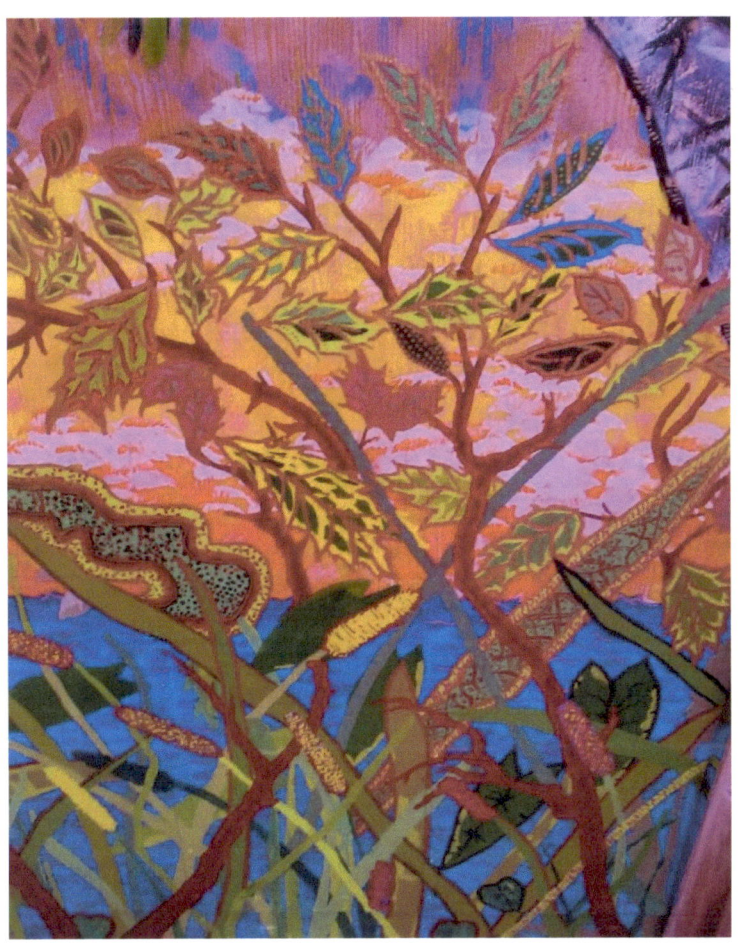

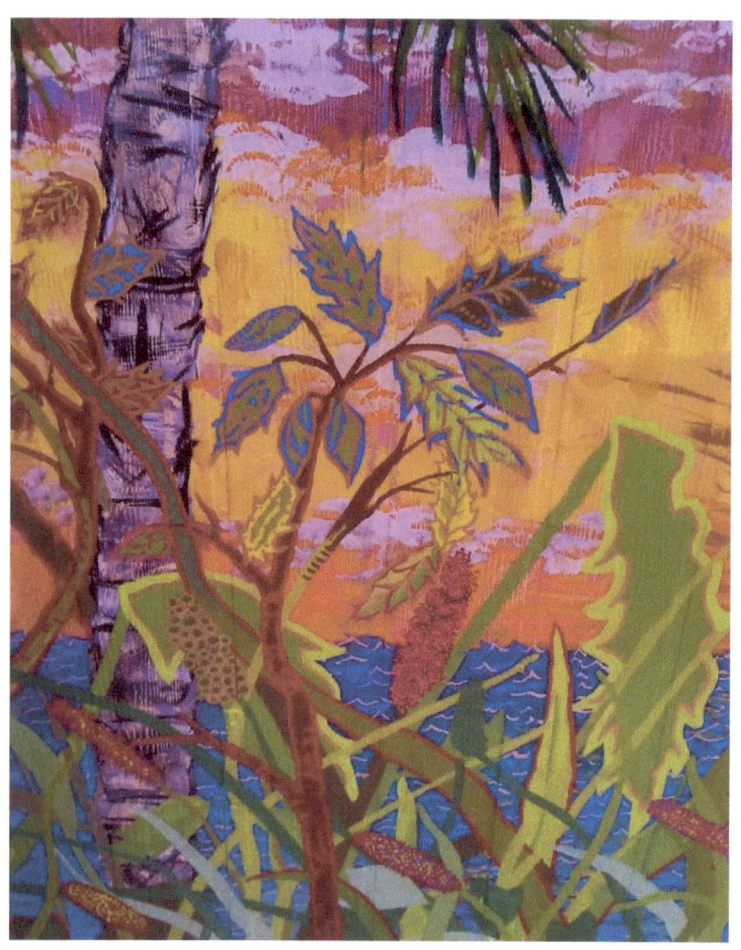

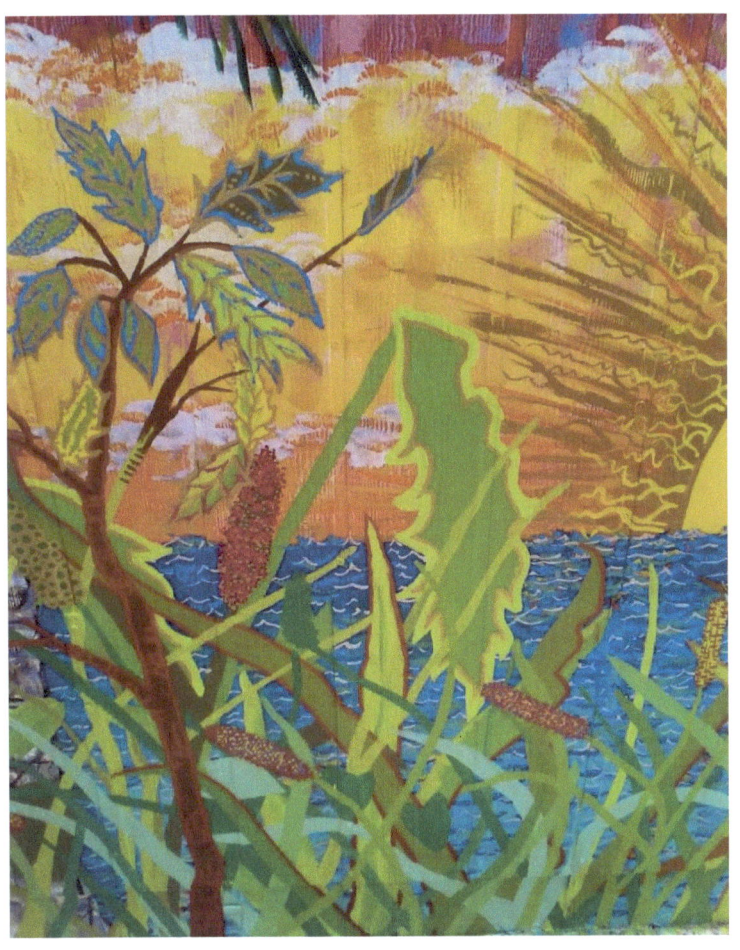

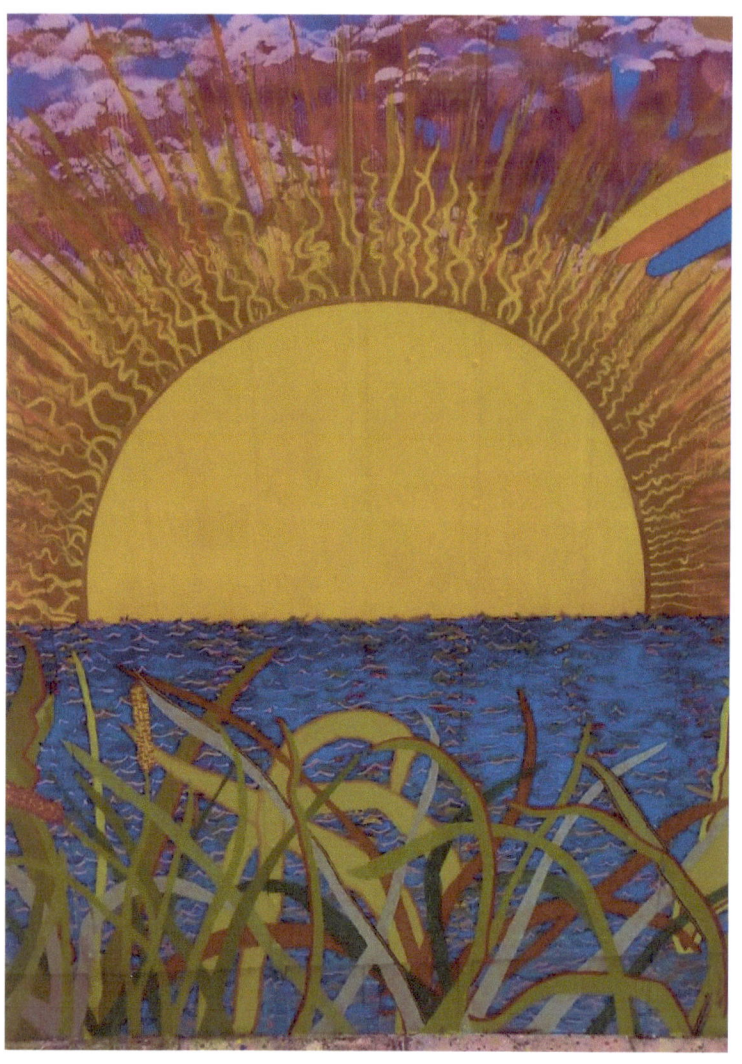

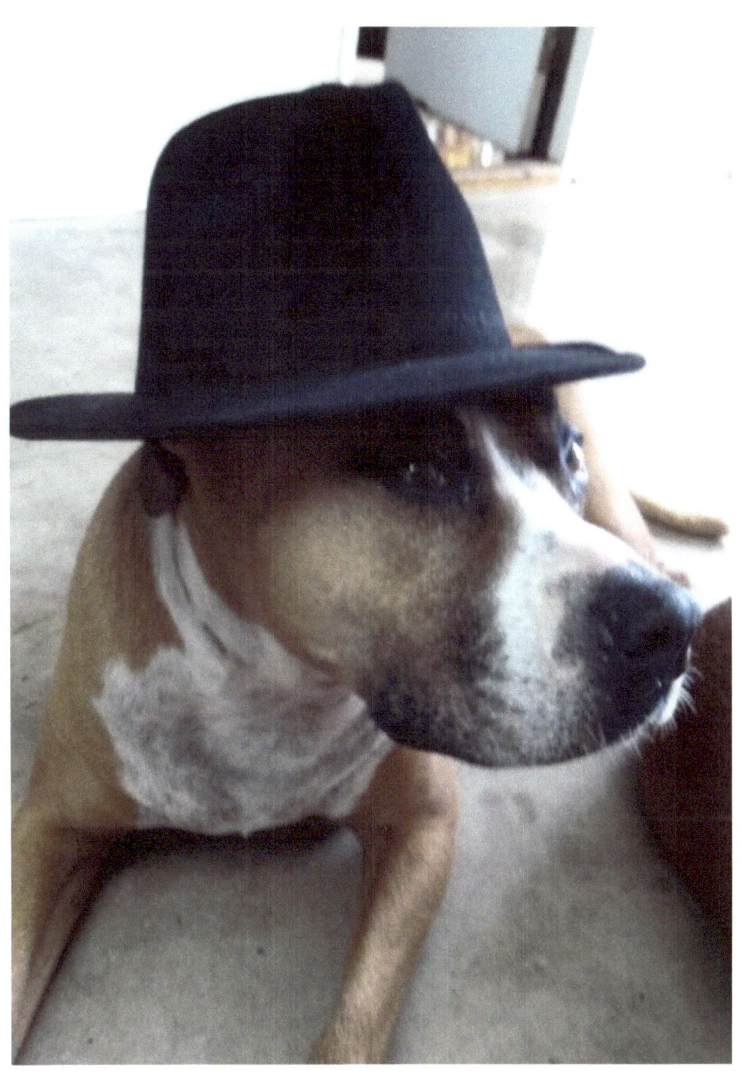

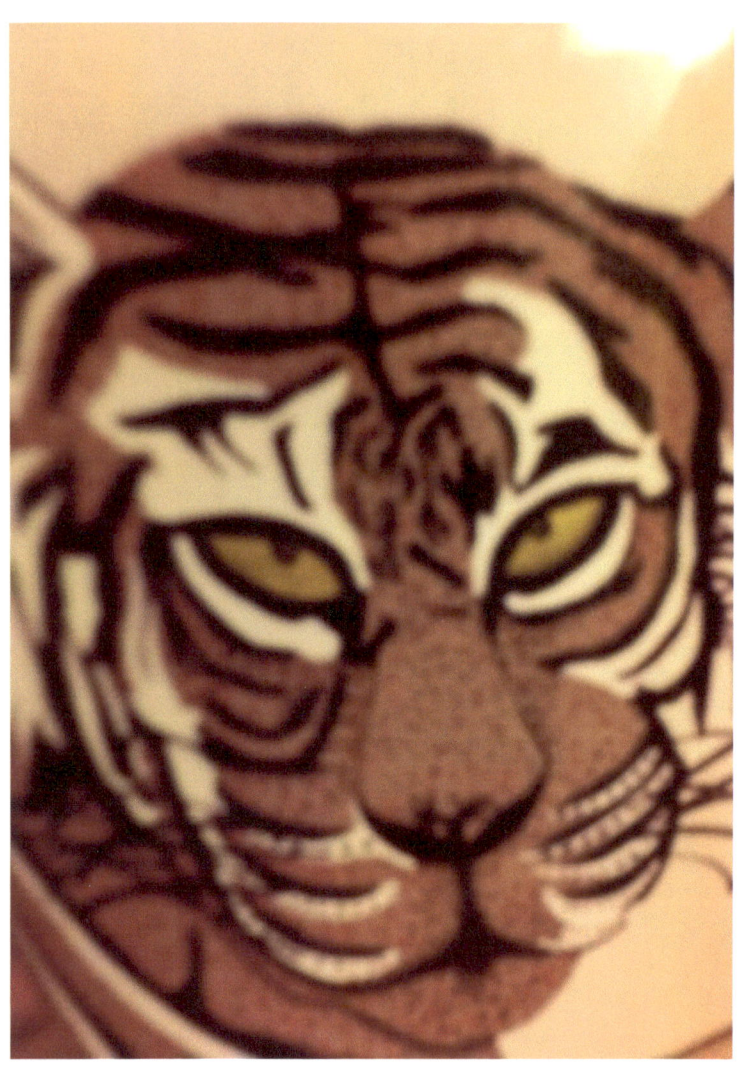

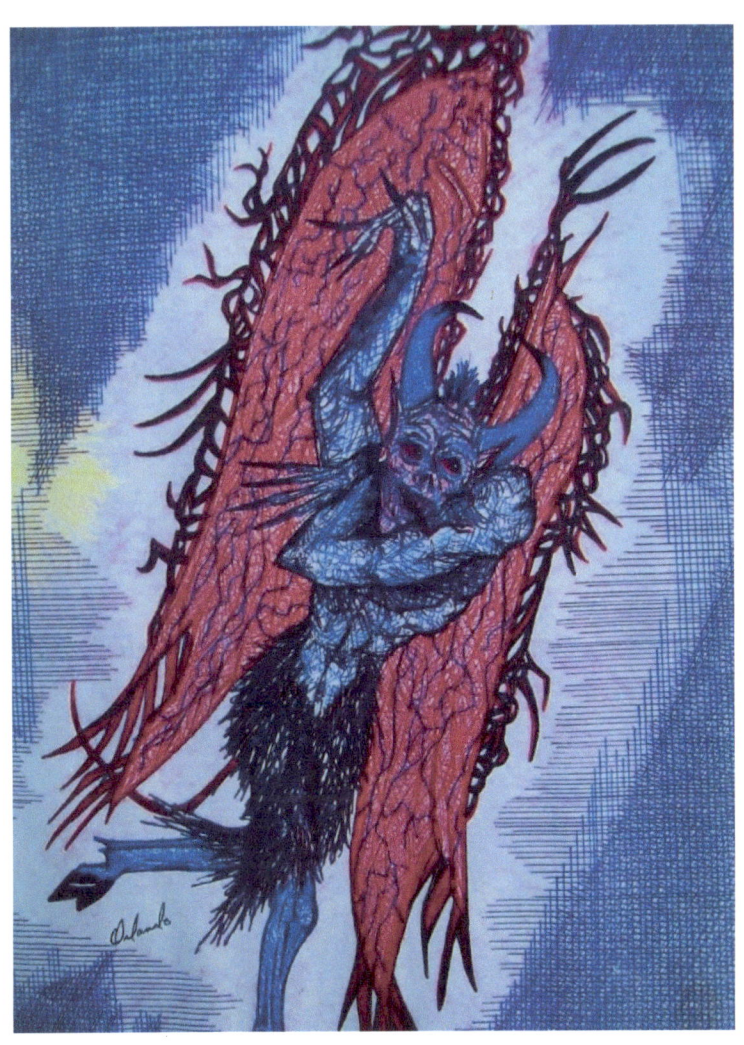

I hope you enjoyed Art Zone. If so, I would appreciate it if you would leave a review on the website where you purchased the book.

If you are interested in murals, photography, props or custom decorating of any sort, commercial or residential, please contact me at 239-234-0637.

Orlando Hernandez

My Political Cartoons

First Book – Vol. 1
First Book – Vol. 2

www.ingramcontent.com/pod-product-compliance
Lightning Source LLC
Chambersburg PA
CBHW040834180526
45159CB00001B/181